This book is an extraordinary balance of personal experience and biblical principle. For those who believe the Holy Spirit lives in and speaks through every believer, this book helps you wade through the mass of opinion and discern what is profitable for edification. And for those who are skeptical that the Spirit still speaks today, you will at least appreciate the way Michael Sullivant stands with both feet firmly planted on the inspired Word of God.

—Floyd McClung, Senior Pastor
Metro Christian Fellowship, Kansas City, Missouri

Michael Sullivant possesses a rare gifting of wisdom and understanding. He is no "swivel-chair theologian," but one who has learned in the trenches of everyday experience. God has granted Michael the ability to unravel many of the "mysteries" involved in understanding the prophetic realm. This book is a must for anyone involved in the prophetic ministry.

—David Ravenhill, Author and Teacher
Lindale, Texas

We are in the days of the "sons and daughters prophesying." Michael stands as a maturing prophetic minister with knowledge, revelation, experience and compassion to help bring these "sons and daughters" into men and women. May the family of God sit around the table and exercise proper etiquette befitting King's kids!

—Steve Witt, Senior Pastor
Metro Church South, Berea, Ohio

This book is a necessity for all who believe God still desires to speak to and through His people today. It is deeply profound and highly practical, calling us to maturity and accountability in an area of ministry that has been misused and misunderstood.

—Robert Stearns, Executive Director
Eagles' Wings Ministries, New York, New York

Michael Sullivant is a man with a passion for and a dedication to seeing the ministry of the revelatory gifts promoted and demonstrated according to guidelines put forth in Scripture. As an end result, God receives His glory and human lives are changed.

—Tom Davis, Founder and President
Amber Rose Ministries

The Lord has prepared Michael's life and ministry to set the stage for this clear practical presentation of truth for the church of the new millennium. This book is not about theory. It comes from a life prepared by the Master, which gives Michael the authority to speak directly and compassionately to both present and future prophetic ministers and to the body of Christ.

—Larry Kreider, International Director
DOVE Christian Fellowship International

Etiquette is discipline mixed with grace. It is self-imposed boundaries that prevent mistakes and misunderstandings while encouraging partnerships of mutual accountability and supernatural power. There are few people who could write this book. Michael is one who models in himself the requirements about which he writes. It will be required reading in all my schools.

—*Graham Cooke, Author*
Developing Your Prophetic Gifting *and*
A Divine Confrontation

We now have brought to the table a book on prophetic ministry with a unique blend of wisdom, experiential understanding and revelatory light. *Prophetic Etiquette* by my friend Michael Sullivant has a distinctive mentoring quality woven throughout. It is a must-read for anyone desiring to advance in the perilous path of prophetic maturation.

—*Jim W. Goll, Director*
Ministry to the Nations
Author of The Lost Art of Intercession *and*
Kneeling on the Promises

God is raising up prophetic voices to arouse His people to a new passion for Him. Yet great care and wisdom is needed to navigate this "prophetic" terrain, and there are few who can do so as adeptly as Michael Sullivant. Sullivant has the heart of a prophet and the mind of a teacher—one who can embrace all God is doing, yet is firmly rooted within sound biblical parameters.

—*Steve Fry, Recording Artist*
Founder and President, Messenger Fellowship
Brentwood, Tennessee

There are many prophetic ministries in operation today, but few are as well suited to write such a book as Michael Sullivant has written. Michael is not only a prophetic voice, but he is also, and much more importantly, a man of godliness. Michael is not a wild-eyed fanatic, but rather a prophetic teacher of wisdom, encouragment and life. Michael demonstrates that all-important lesson that many prophets never learn: "The prophet is the prophecy; the messenger is the message."

—*Marc DuPont*
Prophetic Teacher and Author

Prophetic Etiquette addresses an issue relevant to the whole body of Christ. It is practical, informative, insightful and compelling in its arguments for the prophetic and the work of the Holy Spirit in the world today. I will be encouraging every member of our congregation to read this book.

—*Howard Cordell, Pastor*
Faith Covenant House of Prayer, Kansas City, Missouri

Proper prophetic etiquette is more than good manners—though spiritual civility is often missing and is certainly welcome. Prophetic etiquette, as Michael Sullivant explains it, is the very pipeline that allows the Spirit to flow. This isn't a discourse on niceties; this is a manual on spiritual mechanics.

—*John L. Moore, Journalist and Prophetic Minister*
Author of award-winning novel The Breaking of Ezra Riley

PROPHETIC
ETIQUETTE

MICHAEL SULLIVANT

PROPHETIC ETIQUETTE by Michael Sullivant
Published by Creation House
A division of Strang Communications Company
600 Rinehart Road
Lake Mary, Florida 32746
www.creationhouse.com

Unless otherwise noted, all Scripture quotations are from
the New King James Version of the Bible. Copyright ©
1979, 1980, 1982 by Thomas Nelson, Inc., publishers.
Used by permission.

Scripture quotations marked NAS are from the New
American Standard Bible. Copyright © 1960, 1962, 1963,
1968, 1971, 1972, 1973, 1975, 1977 by the Lockman
Foundation. Used by permission.

Scripture quotations marked NIV are from the Holy Bible,
New International Version. Copyright © 1973, 1978,
1984, International Bible Society. Used by permission.

Library of Congress Catalog Card Number: 99-85853
International Standard Book Number: 0-88419-675-5

0 1 2 3 4 5 VP 8 7 6 5 4 3 2 1
Printed in the United States of America

To my precious children: Luke, Lisa, Samuel, Michael and Stephen. I can only marvel at whom each of you is becoming as you are offering all that you are back to the worship and service of God. How can five people from the same gene pool be so uniquely different? You are shining lights to all that know you. My love and respect for each one of you continue to grow richer through the years. You have made me a truly wealthy man. You are in the powerful and loving grip of One much greater than your mother or I. Forge ahead—I'll try to keep up!

> Behold, children are a heritage from the LORD, the fruit of the womb is a reward. Like arrows in the hand of a warrior, so are the children of one's youth. Happy is the man who has his quiver full of them; they shall not be ashamed, but shall speak with their enemies in the gate.
>
> —PSALM 127:3–5

CONTENTS

FOREWORD

MICHAEL SULLIVANT HAS offered to the body of Christ a very valuable and important book on a subject with which he has become intimately acquainted. I know this because I have been tracking his spiritual journey for over twenty years and have now walked closely with him in ministry for almost thirteen years. This book has been birthed out of many years of personal intensive study of and meditation upon the Scriptures, careful observations of other prophetically gifted people and deep partnerships with those who lead and pastor local churches, personal prophetic experiences and the practical experience of nurturing and governing prophetic ministry within our church, Metro Christian Fellowship. In the preface to my book *Growing in the Prophetic,* which Michael coauthored with me, I stated, "He is more than qualified to write his own book on prophetic ministry." Now here it is!

This book first serves to set forth a grand vision of the

joining together of the ministries of the Word of God and the Spirit of God. A passionate hope is rising within the hearts of fervent believers worldwide to see these two elements deeply integrated in the life and lifestyle of the body of Christ. Second, this book convincingly communicates the value of genuine prophetic ministry and experience. Third, it gives penetrating and gracious warnings and cautions about the misuse of "prophetic ministry." Fourth, it recommends four fundamental values that need to be set in place within both individuals and communities that desire to cultivate a holy and helpful expression of prophetic ministry. Fifth, it builds faith for and casts an exciting and sobering vision of what may lie ahead for the body of Christ and gives us insight as to how to prepare and posture ourselves to cooperate with the Holy Spirit as He moves in unprecedented ways on planet earth. Finally, and maybe most profoundly of all, it grants us an intimate peek into Michael's heart processes and how he has been "working out" his own salvation "with fear and trembling" before the Lord and others (Phil. 2:12). He writes to us as a learner as well as a leader. Be warned—you might come under some personal conviction as you read this book!

I also must say that Michael is truly one of my dearest and most trusted friends. God has used his example and ministry to touch and change my life deeply. In all kinds of circumstances he has consistently demonstrated to me and to many others the love of the Father, the character of Christ and the humility, boldness and gifting of the Holy Spirit. He and his precious wife, Terri, not only have forged a marvelous partnership in marriage and ministry, they have also successfully imparted to their five children, with obvious help from above, the very same personal integrity and passion for Jesus that radiate from them both.

I highly recommend *Prophetic Etiquette* to leaders and pastors, prophetic people in every stage of growth, to less prophetic members of the body of Christ and even to the unchurched—there are some who have yet to come to faith in Jesus Christ who just might be "strangely warned" by reading this fascinating book. It is more than a book on the prophetic ministry—it is a book about God Himself, His ways and His kingdom that has application to every dimension of human life and relationships.

—Mike Bickle
Kansas City, Missouri

*P*ROPHETIC ETIQUETTE IS not only a book that I am more than a little happy to see written, but it is a concept and spiritual value that is truly needed among both individuals and groups that are hungry for a higher quality of prophetic ministry. Genuine prophetic ministry has always been, and is today, vital to the effecting of God's purposes upon the earth. There seems to be a shocking absence of genuine dignity, integrity, spiritual poise and theological astuteness coming together with the anointing of the Holy Spirit in those who minister prophetically. My good friend Michael Sullivant has been conscientiously submitting himself to our Lord Jesus Christ and his fellow leaders over many years so that this blending can occur in his life and ministry.

Michael has gained a most valuable kind of practical wisdom that comes from understanding the Scriptures and personal experience. He has a special way of making complex ideas simple without being simplistic. He has earned the right to speak with conviction on this subject that requires both the fear of the Lord and a strong love for people that doesn't get watered down into a fear of man. Only intimacy with the Holy Spirit and the deep dealings of God can work this kind of balance into human souls. Michael's experience in many different aspects of Christian leadership—pastoring, teaching, church planting, management, intercessory ministry and evangelism—have provided a unique and solid base from which his prophetic ministry is growing. As you read, you will be able to perceive and appreciate the peculiar vantage point from which he teaches and exhorts us. He is not falsely humble about his gifting and experience, but he is transparent about his struggles and failures.

God has given Michael special insight into how the prophetic gifts and the power dimension of the Spirit's ministry in general relate to the message of the cross—the heart of the gospel of Jesus Christ. This is a theme for which I share a similar passion. I have come to truly appreciate him as a trustworthy friend, a coworker in the gospel and a profitable spiritual son in the ministry. I hope that you will read and incorporate the truths set forth in this excellent overview of New Testament prophetic ministry. Some things passed off as "prophetic" to the body of Christ have almost caused me to want to distance myself from anything carrying this label. *Prophetic Etiquette* is the kind of work that renews my hope. I believe that it will do the same for many of you.

—PAUL CAIN
SHILOH MINISTRIES
KANSAS CITY, MISSOURI

PREFACE

*P*ROPHETIC ETIQUETTE HAS grown out of a number of years of biblical research and prayerful reflection, quiet observations, intense involvement, international controversies, divine dealings, personal relationships, spiritual encounters, trials and errors, hard work and a few modest successes. I am confident that it is not a perfect book, and therefore I would beg mercy from my readers ahead of time for any of its failures and/or imbalances. Those would be all mine and should in no way be blamed on our Lord.

I have loved the written Word of God since the time of my conversion to Christ in 1973. I have also loved the ways and movements of the Holy Spirit who makes the Scriptures "come alive" in our hearts and lives, and who provides us with joy and conviction upon our journey. I pray that this book will inspire a similar and greater love for both in those who will read it.

God is pouring out a prophetic spirit upon the body of

Christ on a grand and global scale in our generation. This will prove to be no small event in human history. God will utilize the power of prophecy to actually help trigger the last-day biblical scenarios that will culminate in the return of Jesus Christ to earth. This move of the Holy Spirit has really just begun to pick up momentum. The prophetic anointing to which the body of Christ at large is being reintroduced is not going away. However, we can hinder it, or we can see that it is fanned into a more intense flame of love, power and wisdom.

Churches, church leaders and Christians are in need of a clear set of encouragements and warnings regarding prophetic ministry that is both faithful to Scripture and that effectively translates into practical experience for normal Christian life. Certain believers who are being specifically called into prophetic ministry need to have a pathway defined for them—or at least outlined to some degree. We also need to understand how prophetic experience fits into the broader context of Christian experience and day-to-day healthy church life. Many other prophetic leaders, pastors and Bible teachers have made some important contributions to this end, and I can only pray that aspects of this book will add to the growing body of wisdom on this very important subject.

This book is not about five, seven, ten or twelve "guaranteed easy steps into an anointed prophetic ministry" that any average Christian can achieve in her or his spare time. It does recommend some basic values that need to be internalized, and it provides some general guidelines that will hopefully help to transfer some of our internal heat into visible light! It is more about living a life before God and others in such a way that we will be postured to receive all that our gracious Lord intends for any one of us. God is desirous of telling a special story to all creation through each of our lives. I am asking the Lord that the teachings and testimonies in this book will help others perceive some points they may have overlooked in the divine drama of their journey in God.

I have desired to significantly write out of my personal experience in contrast to the experience of others. I have included a number of testimonies of prophetic experiences that represent spiritual victories for me. I want to give the glory to God for the gracious and undeserved blessings of these events and encounters. I don't apologize for them, but I rather "boast in the Lord" concerning them. At the same time, I hope that the accounts of my failures and struggles will also serve to honor the Lord and encourage my readers. It would require a whole volume in itself just to catalog them!

There are sections of the book that are quite intense, but I am not sure how to say some of these things with less zeal. I can only trust that the Spirit of the Lord will use this rather penetrating mode of speech. I could say, "Please don't take the hard sayings so personally," but I would be less than honest if I did. I have. I hope you do!

I want to thank Creation House's director of product development, Rick Nash, for seeking me out to write this book. My old college buddy David Welday (vice president of product development at Creation House) also helped to get the ball rolling on this project—I'm grateful for our reconnection, Dave. Barbara Dycus, my editor, has been most helpful in the process of bringing this book to completion.

I am indebted to my colleague and friend of over twenty years, Mike Bickle, who has entrusted me with so many things valuable to him. God will use him as a mighty reformer in the body of Christ across many nations—it has already begun. I also want to honor Paul Cain for his profound example to me and to a whole generation of hungry believers—you have led the way well, dear friend of God. My ministry teammates and the whole staff of Metro Christian Fellowship have continually honored me and encouraged me to obey the Lord. Thank you, dear men and women. My father, Wayne, since my truly awesome mother and his precious wife went to heaven in 1989, has taken up the assignment to intercede for my family and me day and night. Few men in my generation have been so blessed by their fathers.

Most of all, I want to thank my marvelous wife, Terri. God has used her more than any other earthly person to stimulate my spiritual growth. Not only does she intensely love God with her whole being, but He has also anointed her to inspire, instruct and challenge me through profound prophetic revelations that have been shot like arrows of light and truth into my heart on countless occasions. It's unsettling, but in a good way, to live with someone who not only knows you so well, but who also hears from God about the secrets of your heart! Still, she has accepted and believed in me for these twenty-three years. She has stood with me in my times of weakness and discouragement. She has rejoiced when I have been honored above her. She has joyfully sacrificed her time and energies and significantly spent her gifts upon the nurturing of our five children for the last twenty-one years of her life. She is a wife and mother of rare beauty and excellence. Additionally, she has been involved in touching the lives of so many others beyond our family and her own parents and siblings. However, Terri Sullivant's real public ministry has hardly begun, so watch out! Her hour is swiftly approaching.

THE WEDDING OF TRUTH AND EXPERIENCE

S OME YEARS AGO while in prayer during a ministry trip in Germany, I received a vision. I saw a large, beautiful flagpole planted in the foreground of an outdoor scene. A strong wind was blowing, and the trees in the background were being affected powerfully by the wind. The flagpole stood majestically—unmoved by the wind. I heard a voice say, "What's missing?"

"Lord," I replied, "there is no flag." Then at the base of this great flagpole, I saw a plain package appear.

Suddenly, the wrapper at the bottom of the pole was supernaturally undone, and I saw a multicolored flag emerge from it, hoisted upward without the assistance of human hands. As it rose, the wind caught the resilient yet delicate fabric, and the flag quickly unfurled, flapping strongly and gracefully in the wind. It seemed as though the whole world could see this awesome banner.

I noticed the contrast between the flagpole and the

flag. The flagpole was steel-like, silent and unbending. The flag was attention grabbing and highly responsive to the wind. Both of them were dazzling in their own ways.

While I was having this vision, I understood by the Holy Spirit that the flagpole and flag were pictures of two sides of our Christian faith—the objective side and the subjective side. The objective, essential, historically proven truths and doctrines of our faith are stable, plain, unchanging, firmly grounded and established—they are fundamental and vital as they shine forth. The subjective, experiential aspects of our life in the Spirit of God are more delicate, visible and fluid—they inspire passion, enthusiasm and flair. I heard that voice say, "What's a flagpole without a flag? But then again, what's a flag without a flagpole? It's good for nothing except to be cast down and trampled upon by men of the earth."

I believe that God is working in our day to bring together these two aspects of our faith into a dynamic duo—complementary elements of a unified whole. So often in the history of the church and her movements each side has had its champions who unwittingly neglected or even denigrated the other vital side. This ought not to be. What God has joined together let not man divide. The objective ministry of the written Word of God and the subjective ministry of the Holy Spirit go together—like spoken words and the breath that attends them.

> By the word of the LORD the heavens were made, and
> all the host of them by the breath [spirit] of His mouth.
> —PSALM 33:6

It is essential to remember that the objective truths of Scripture that we know and build our lives upon were once subjectively communicated by God to humanity. The divine reality and veracity of these experiences were objectified by "passing the tests" of their universal and enduring impact and the corroborating witness of credible people who knew and loved God. By this God has provided us with a reliable measuring rod to evaluate other subjective experiences that claim divine inspiration as their source.

A MORE SURE WORD—CONNECTING
EXPERIENCE WITH THE SCRIPTURES

In 2 Peter, Peter refers to a powerful, personal "prophetic" experience and explains how he viewed it in relationship to the Old Testament Scriptures.

> For we did not follow cunningly devised fables when we made known to you the power and coming of our Lord Jesus Christ, but were eyewitnesses of His majesty. For He received from God the Father honor and glory when such a voice came to Him from the Excellent Glory: "This is My beloved Son, in whom I am well pleased." And we heard this voice which came from heaven when we were with Him on the holy mountain.
>
> And so we have the prophetic word confirmed, which you do well to heed as a light that shines in a dark place, until the day dawns and the morning star rises in your hearts; knowing this first, that no prophecy of Scripture is of any private interpretation, for prophecy never came by the will of man, but holy men of God spoke as they were moved by the Holy Spirit.
>
> —2 PETER 1:16–21

Ironically, this very account of Peter's experience on the Mount of Transfiguration ultimately became a part of the Holy Scriptures. Without apology or false humility, he speaks about what he saw and heard when the supernatural power of God was demonstrated on the mountain. (See Matthew 17:1–9.) Peter utilized this testimony as a part of his preaching of the gospel as he sought to persuade people to put their faith in Jesus and to build up believers in their faith in Jesus. But he also refers to the "prophetic word" of Scripture itself and implies that it must stand as the superior, "more sure" and "confirmed" prophetic revelation of God through which we are to evaluate any subjective supernatural experiences.

Far from being down on experience, Peter is simply appealing for us always to ground our experiences by evaluating them in the light of the objectified truths of the Bible itself—just as he did himself. If this method and attitude was good enough for Peter, it should certainly be good enough for us!

If we are firmly grounded in the objective side of our faith we need not fear welcoming the subjective experiential side of our faith. We need not fear being deceived by experience. Christians have often attributed more ability to Satan to deceive us than to the Holy Spirit to lead us into truth. Deception is certainly possible, but it is not inevitable. Two reliable internal safeguards against deception are the continual receiving into our hearts of the "love of the truth" whenever God's truth intersects our lives and orienting ourselves to find and pursue our life's pleasures in God and the things of His kingdom. This is the essence of possessing *integrity*. If these two things are not firmly in place within us, then we are indeed in great danger of being deceived in one way or another. Both the

Book of Proverbs and the apostle Paul warn us soberly about the absolute need for such integrity:

> He who walks with integrity walks securely.
>
> —PROVERBS 10:9

> The integrity of the upright will guide them, but the perversity of the unfaithful will destroy them.
>
> —PROVERBS 11:3

> The coming of the lawless one is according to the working of Satan, with all power, signs, and lying wonders, and with all unrighteous deception among those who perish, because they did not receive the love of the truth, that they might be saved. And for this reason God will send them strong delusion, that they should believe the lie, that they all may be condemned who did not believe the truth but had pleasure in unrighteousness.
>
> —2 THESSALONIANS 2:9–12

Notice that it is actually God Himself who allows these people to be deluded because they have rejected Him as the legitimate source of pleasure in this life. At its root, deception is a moral—not an intellectual—problem.

Before we move on, it is important to become clear about the proper and improper ways of *seeking pleasure*.

A BIBLICAL VIEW OF "PLEASURE"

Despite the danger of being "lovers of pleasure rather than lovers of God" (2 Tim. 3:4), God really is not "down" on pleasure. In fact, He is the originator of every legitimate pleasure.

You will show me the path of life; in Your presence is fullness of joy; at Your right hand are pleasures forevermore.

—PSALM 16:11

How precious is Your lovingkindness, O God! Therefore the children of men put their trust under the shadow of Your wings. They are abundantly satisfied with the fullness of Your house, and You give them drink from the river of Your pleasures.

—PSALM 36:7–8

The highest and deepest pleasures available to a human being are the *transcendent pleasures* that come from personally connecting with God and His kingdom: forgiveness of sins, love, peace, joy, righteousness, hope, intimate communion and worship and the power dimension of the Holy Spirit's ministry. These realities, and many others like them, are substantially available to us here and now and will be fully realized in the age to come. Our desire to experience the happiness that comes from these things is a *God-given instinct* from which we should not, and truly cannot, repent. No human has ever successfully repented from her or his desire for true happiness—despite the railings of misguided religionists through the centuries. You will not be the first person to succeed at turning away from this motivation, and neither will I! We might as well cease the attempt to do so and capitalize upon this basic legitimate longing for the glory of God.

The pursuit of these pleasures is not an exercise in selfishness or carnal self-indulgence. Indeed, God *commands* us to seek after them with zeal and passion:

Delight yourself also in the LORD, and He shall give
you the desires of your heart.

—PSALM 37:4

God is the one who has designed us for genuine delight.
He is most glorified in and through our lives when we
heartily pursue this kind of transcendent pleasure. It is
right for us to be lovers of the pleasure that is found in
God. This above verse from the Book of Psalms is simply
another way of saying, "Believe on the Lord Jesus Christ,
and you shall be saved." Our desire for personal salvation
is not selfish. In fact, we are commanded to receive it as a
free gift from God. Doing so blesses His heart and glorifies
Him as the great Giver that He is. As we delight ourselves
in God, He works to purify our hearts' desires in the
process. God can then legitimately satisfy *those* desires.

In addition to transcendent pleasures, God has also
ordained *earthly pleasures* for our enjoyment and delight:

Command those who are rich in this present age not
to be haughty, nor to trust in uncertain riches but in
the living God, *who gives us richly all things to enjoy.*
—1 TIMOTHY 6:17, EMPHASIS ADDED

I would call these pleasures the *simple pleasures* of
human life. Imagine for a moment the past pleasures you
have experienced—including noble work and a job well
done, a good meal, a good book, a good game, the
beauty of nature, a good drama, a beautiful song, a good
friend, a good deal, a warm fire on a cold night, sex
within marriage, bearing children, watching your child's
personality develop, an affectionate hug, a good night's
sleep, a Sunday afternoon nap, a faithful pet, gazing on

the ocean or the mountains, a long walk on a beautiful day, a fresh snow and a refreshing rain.

When we experience these kinds of legitimate pleasures in the midst of this sinful age, we are called to trace the joy we feel back to the One who has given them to us to enjoy. When we then express our *gratitude* to God for the pleasure they bring to us, we are glorifying Him as God—the source of all true pleasure. This kind of celebration within our hearts brings pleasure to His heart. He's happy that we are happy, and we are happy that He is happy that we are happy! This is what can be called "happy holiness"—a holiness that reflects the sublime happiness that God enjoys within Himself as a sweet trinitarian society. God both loves and likes who He is and what He has done, and He would be and do the same all over again! Any sadness or anger He experiences happens within the context of His greater divine self-satisfaction. A lesser God would truly not be worthy of our worship.

True happiness is not a limited commodity in this universe. We don't have to strive and grasp for our little piece of it and protect it for all we are worth. Rather, happiness is like a *glorious virus*. And we are called to be "carriers." One day the whole universe will be fully infected, and there will be no cure. In light of this, receiving from God and others is good and holy; if it weren't, then giving would be a sin. In giving we multiply our own happiness, which is also good and holy. For as marvelous as it is to receive, it is even *"more blessed* [i.e., it makes us even more *happy]* to *give* than to *receive."* (Compare and combine Matthew 10:8 with Acts 20:35.)

We are not called to make ourselves sad in order to make others happy. If our giving something to a loved one would make us sad, then it would demean the whole wonderful dynamic of giving. The sacrifice, self-denial and suffering that Jesus and the apostles call us in Scripture to embrace and endure are always with a view to our receiving a greater reward in the end. This basic *reward motivation* is never pictured as selfish or sinful, but God has strategically placed it within us, and He wants to capitalize upon it for His glory and our greater happiness. God has designed the universe and all within it to *thrive* on giving and receiving. If only humanity would line up with this divine principle of life. This indeed is the brilliant appeal of the gospel of Jesus Christ to a human race in bondage to grasping and taking.

The real complicating problem with earthly pleasures is that they, rather than God Himself, can gradually become the *focus* of our heart's passions. When this happens, earthly pleasures become *sinful pleasures*. What God intends to be *subordinate* becomes *dominant,* and this makes them *inordinate*—something good is taken "out of bounds," and it becomes evil. This is the essence of idolatry—we take what is created and remake it into an object of worship. In the process of this idolatry, the worship of God is neglected and displaced, and our fellowship with Him is cut off.

Satan has never created anything. He is only able to manipulate the things that God has created and twist them into sinful expressions. He is a master counterfeiter. He has done this very thing with pleasure. There is a warped kind of "pleasure" in sin; otherwise it would never be tempting to us. (See Hebrews 11:25.) The primary strategy of the evil one is to *morph* true pleasures into sinful expressions and deceive us into believing that experiencing these sinful pleasures will make us happier than we are without indulging in them.

9

The bottom line is that it is not our pursuit of pleasure that is wrong; it is the foolish way that we humans so often go about pursuing pleasure. We are deceived by the deceitfulness of sin. The temptation of sin is that it promises us satisfaction and happiness if we buy in, but it never delivers the goods. Yet, people become addicted to the fleeting "highs" of inferior pleasures—the expression of the *sinful passions* of the human heart, mind and body. If they could only taste and see how good the Lord is, they would joyfully forsake the control of these sinful passions and unleash their deeper passion to "experience God." The true "high life" is life in the Holy Spirit:

> And do not be drunk with wine, in which is dissipation; but be filled with the Spirit.
> —EPHESIANS 5:18

The reason that I have included this section about pleasure is because the proper pursuit of hearing from and personally interacting with God can be extremely pleasurable to our souls. I want to remove any false guilt lurking about our thinking over this fact here at the start. We will encounter many people along the way, some well intentioned, who will call this pursuit an exercise in prideful, spiritual self-indulgence. If they only knew! Exploring the prophetic ministry of the Holy Spirit can be a truly spiritually intoxicating enterprise. Yet I believe that it will also greatly glorify the Lord Jesus Christ and adorn His good news through the church among the nations.

Incidentally, it is not only those who welcome subjective spiritual experiences who can fall into deception. If we lack experience, build justifying doctrines around this lack and attempt to impart the fear of deception to anyone who might be open to or hungry for experiences with God, then we are already trapped in and propagating a terrible deception.

This dynamic principle is well illustrated by the spiritual condition of the Sadducees of Jesus' day. They fell into serious theological error not only because of their inaccurate interpretations and applications of the Scriptures, but also by their bias against and denial of the power of God. Because they lacked a philosophical grid for the supernatural, they stumbled badly over the glaring reality of a life-altering future experience that awaited them and awaits us all—the resurrection to a life beyond this earthly life.

> Then some Sadducees, who say there is no resurrection, came to Him; and they asked Him, saying: "Teacher, Moses wrote to us that if a man's brother dies, and leaves his wife behind, and leaves no children, his brother should take his wife and raise up offspring for his brother. Now there were seven brothers. The first took a wife; and dying, he left no offspring. And the second took her, and he died; nor did he leave any offspring. And the third likewise. So the seven had her and left no offspring. Last of all the woman died also. Therefore, in the resurrection, when they rise, whose wife will she be? For all seven had her as wife."
>
> Jesus answered and said to them, "Are you not therefore mistaken, because you do not know the Scriptures nor the power of God? For when they rise from the dead, they neither marry nor are given in marriage, but are like angels in heaven. But concerning the dead, that they rise, have you not read

11

in the book of Moses, in the burning bush passage, how God spoke to him, saying, 'I am the God of Abraham, the God of Isaac, and the God of Jacob'? He is not the God of the dead, but the God of the living. You are therefore greatly mistaken."

—MARK 12:18–27

If we do not make room in our thinking for the demonstration of God's miraculous power among humanity, then we will also misinterpret the Scriptures, be greatly mistaken about many of God's ways and be unable truly to live and walk by faith in the ways that God has intended us to live and walk.

Chapter 1

A Spiritual Paradigm Shift

A PARADIGM SHIFT IS occurring rapidly across the body of Christ throughout the world. A biblical worldview is being reestablished, one that includes Christians receiving and ministering the supernatural gifts of the Holy Spirit in our day. Cessationism, which contends that the miraculous "sign gifts" of the Spirit passed away with the passing of the first apostles of Jesus in the first century, is ceasing. Cessationism has been a popular belief system in the Western world among many conservative theologians and church movements throughout the last century or so. But the arguments upon which it is built are deeply flawed, and they lack intellectual as well as spiritual integrity. Because of that, many biblical scholars are abandoning their belief in cessationism.

There are two basic reasons that cessationism took hold in the body of Christ. First, in various Christian circles it has served as an explanation for a lack of experience of the supernatural power of God. Its followers reason: "We know that we are genuine Christians. The Holy Spirit lives in us, and *we've* never seen supernatural gifts operate in our group(s), so therefore these gifts *must* have ceased." Second, it has served to warn and protect some Christian groups from the abuses and extremes of other religious movements that embraced a belief in supernatural ministry and experience. The first reason is a *rationalization,* and the second is an *overreaction.* As a result of such thinking, Bible passages have been twisted and given strange interpretations to fit these prejudices in an attempt to "prove" that cessationism is biblical.

But many scholars are seeing through the faulty worldview and scriptural interpretations behind cessationism. The testimonies of a growing number of credible witnesses have been pouring in from all over the world giving credence to the ongoing nature and manifestation of God's miraculous power in and through the church. Many of these reports are coming from people who themselves have been committed cessationists. Since the turn of the century, over four hundred million people have been ushered into some kind of personal experience with the supernatural power of the Holy Spirit through the Pentecostal/Charismatic/Third-Wave movements within the body of Christ. This has been the fastest-growing people movement in the history of the world. The biblical and testimonial evidences of the validity and reality of God's miraculous works within our generation are overwhelming any ideas to the contrary. It almost seems that God is enjoying breaking out of the confining theological box in which some of His children have placed Him!

In this chapter you will meet one of these people. Here

we present a marvelous personal testimony of how God is moving in our generation to convince sincere and highly intelligent, but theologically conservative, believers about the power and relevancy of the present-day prophetic ministry of the Holy Spirit through the church.

For the last number of years, I have been blessed to work in very close association with Dr. Sam Storms. Sam is the president of the Grace Training Center in Kansas City and is one of the main pastoral leaders in our fellowship. He, his wife, Ann, their two daughters, Joanna and Melanie, and Melanie's husband, Konrad Liang, are one of the most highly regarded and deeply loved families in our congregation. Beyond this, Sam is highly respected by many contemporary theologians for his biblical scholarship and great theological mind. At one time, Sam had been steeped in cessationism. But he joyfully discovered that God's powerful gifts are still valid and useful in our day—as they have been throughout the centuries. In his own words, Sam shares his journey into the reality of the power dimension of the Holy Spirit's ministry.

MY JOURNEY
(AS TOLD BY DR. SAM STORMS)

The journey my wife and I have been on is also one that has seen its fair share of supernatural phenomena. Until early in 1988 my life and ministry were both uneventful in terms of what one might call overt supernatural activity. Ann and I were married in May of 1972, and we both graduated from the University of Oklahoma in May of 1973. In September of that year I entered Dallas Theological Seminary, from which I received my Th.M. in

15

Historical Theology in 1977. Upon graduation I joined the staff of Believers Chapel, a large independent Bible church in Dallas, and stayed there until August of 1985. During this time I received my Ph.D. in Intellectual History from the University of Texas at Dallas.

My intention had always been to teach in a seminary or graduate institution of some sort. But the Lord had something else in mind. In August of 1985 we moved to Ardmore, Oklahoma, where I became senior pastor of Christ Community Church, an independent Bible church of about two hundred people.

Like virtually all graduates of Dallas Theological Seminary, I was a cessationist. I never questioned the doctrine of cessationism until reading a book by Donald A. Carson titled *Showing the Spirit: A Theological Exposition of 1 Corinthians 12–14* (Baker Book House, 1987). This volume exposed the errors in a number of arguments I had used through the years to defend cessationism. It is important to make clear that I did not reject cessationism because of some spiritual experience or miracle that I witnessed. I rejected cessationism because, in the solitude and safety of my study, I became convinced that the Bible didn't teach it.

Perhaps the most painful part of this particular theological shift was my discovery of the primary reason I had so long resisted the full range of the Spirit's gifts. Beyond the biblical arguments to which I would appeal, I was, quite frankly, embarrassed by the appearance and behavior of many who were associated with spiritual gifts in the public eye. I didn't like the way they dressed. I didn't like the way they spoke. I was offended by their lack of sophistication and their overbearing flamboyance. I was disturbed by their flippant disregard for theological precision and their excessive displays of emotional exuberance.

My opposition to spiritual gifts was also energized by fear: the fear of emotionalism, the fear of fanaticism, the fear of the unfamiliar, the fear of rejection by those whose respect I cherished and whose friendship I did not want to forfeit, the fear of what might occur were I to fully relinquish control of my life and mind and emotions to the Holy Spirit, the fear of losing what little status in the evangelical community that I had worked so hard to attain.

I'm talking about the kind of fear that energized a personal agenda to distance myself from anything that had the potential to link me with people who I believed were an embarrassment to the cause of Christ. I was faithful to the eleventh commandment of Bible church evangelicalism: "Thou shalt not do at all what others do poorly." In my pride I had allowed certain extremists to exercise more of an influence on the shape of my ministry than I did the text of Scripture. Fear of being labeled or linked or in some way associated with the "unlearned" and "unattractive" elements in contemporary Christendom exercised an insidious power on my ability and willingness to be objective in the reading of Holy Scripture. I am not so naive as to think that my understanding of Scripture is now free from subjective influences! But I am confident that at least fear, in this form, no longer plays a part.

By the way, if all this sounds like the arrogance and self-righteousness of someone who prized "being right" above everything else, that's because that's precisely what it was!

Praying in the Spirit

My first encounter with the gifts of the Spirit came when I was nineteen years old, in the summer of 1970. I was living in Lake Tahoe, Nevada, serving with Campus Crusade for Christ on an evangelistic project.

One night I attended a meeting at which Harald Bredesen, one of the early leaders of the Charismatic movement, was scheduled to speak. He mentioned a book by John Sherrill titled *They Speak With Other Tongues*. I bought a copy and read it immediately. The issue of speaking in tongues soon became an obsession with me. As my time of ministry in Tahoe came to end, I returned to the University of Oklahoma to continue my studies. It was during this time I began to pray earnestly that if the gift were real, God would give it to me. For several weeks I spent each night in a secluded area near my fraternity house pleading with God for some indication of His will for me concerning this gift.

One night in October of 1970, quite without warning, I had an experience that I will never forget. I suddenly began speaking words that made no sense whatsoever. I distinctly remember a somewhat detached sensation, as if I were separate from the one speaking. I had never experienced anything remotely similar to that in all my life. I kept thinking to myself, *Sam, what are you saying? Are you speaking in tongues?* I was both frightened and exhilarated. The experience lasted about one minute.

I was confused, but at the same time felt closer to God and He to me than ever before.

I ran back to my fraternity house filled with excitement and called a friend who was on staff with Campus Crusade for Christ. I didn't tell him what had happened, only that I needed to speak with him immediately. Thirty minutes later I sat down in his car and said, "You'll never guess what happened tonight."

"You spoke in tongues, didn't you?" he asked, almost deadpan.

"Yes! It was great. But I don't understand what it means."

This man cared deeply for me and had no intention of offending me or obstructing my Christian growth. But what he said next affected me for years to come. "Sam, you do realize, don't you, that you will have to resign your position as student leader and give up any hope of joining the staff when you graduate. Campus Crusade doesn't permit people who speak in tongues to hold positions of authority. Of course, if you don't do it again, there's no need for us to tell anyone. Everything can be the same as it was before." (My understanding is that Campus Crusade for Christ reversed their policy on spiritual gifts several years ago.)

I was crushed. I remember feebly trying to speak in tongues the next night, but nothing happened. Not wanting to forfeit my position in the ministry on campus, I concluded that it must have been something other than the Holy Spirit. I never thought it was demonic, although many of my friends did. I explained it away as a momentary emotional outburst that I'd be better off forgetting. I rarely spoke of the incident in the years following, fearful of the disdain of my friends who looked with suspicion on anyone remotely associated with or showing interest in the gift of tongues. Needless to say, I didn't speak in tongues again for twenty years!

The power of a friend's prayer

In November of 1990 I was with Jack Deere, author of *Surprised by the Power of the Spirit* and *Surprised by the Voice of God* (Zondervan), in New Orleans at a theology conference. I described my journey and told him about what had happened back in the fall of 1970. He then reminded me of something the apostle Paul said to young Timothy: "And for this reason I remind you to kindle afresh the gift of God which is in you through the laying on of my hands" (2 Tim. 1:6, NAS). Jack then laid hands on me and asked the Lord to kindle afresh in me this gift He had bestowed so many years before.

This verse in 2 Timothy is important. It tells us that one may receive a spiritual gift only to neglect and ignore it. The imagery Paul uses is helpful. He describes a spiritual gift in terms of a flame that needs to be continually fanned. If it is not understood, nurtured and utilized in the way God intended, the once brightly burning flame can be reduced to a smoldering ember. In essence, Paul was advising Timothy, "Take whatever steps you must take: Study, pray, seek God's face, put it into practice, but by all means stoke the fire until that gift returns to its original intensity."

I took Paul's advice to Timothy and applied it to my own case. Every day, if only for a few minutes, I prayed that God would renew what He had given but I had quenched. I prayed that if it were His will I would once more be able to pray in the Spirit, to speak that heavenly language so that I could praise and thank and bless Him. (See 1 Corinthians 14:2, 16–17.) I didn't wait for some sort of divine seizure, but in faith began simply to speak forth the syllables and words that He brought to mind.

Some eight years have passed now since God renewed His precious gift in my life. Praying in the Spirit is certainly not the most important gift. Neither is it a sign of a spirituality or maturity greater than that of those who do not have this particular gift. But if no less a man than the apostle Paul can say, "I thank God, I speak in tongues more than you all" (1 Cor. 14:18, NAS), who am I to despise this blessed gift of God?

Contrary to the caricatures that many have of this gift, it has served only to enhance and deepen my relationship with the Lord Jesus. Believe it or not, I can still tie my shoelaces, balance my checkbook (well, most of the time), drive a car, hold down a job, and I rarely ever drool! I don't mean to be sarcastic, but this particular gift of the Spirit has a terrible public image. For me to reveal to you that I speak in tongues is to run the risk of being perceived as a mindless, spiritually flabby fanatic who periodically mumbles while in a convulsive or hypnotic trance. I can't do much about that except to encourage you to search the Scriptures and seek the face of God.

On the winds of worship
Without question, the most powerful catalyst in my

personal transformation was the discovery of worship. I had always worshiped God. I had always loved music, especially the great hymns of the church. But all too frequently worship for me was little more than singing songs about God. I rarely had any expectation of meeting God or experiencing His presence or engaging my heart with His or of enjoying Him.

For lack of a better way of putting it, I suddenly felt the freedom to enjoy God. I actually felt his presence. I actually felt His pleasure in me. (See Zephaniah 3:17.) I began to sense a power and spiritual intensity that at first was a bit frightening. Although I have always been a romantic and some-what emotional, when it came to worship, especially in a public setting, I was always careful to rein in my emotions. I felt compelled to preserve a measure of so-called "dignity" and "religious sophistication."

But God visited me in worship! As I drew near to Him, He drew near to me (James 4:8). I began to experience an intimacy and warmth of relationship with God that reminded me of Paul's prayer for the Ephesians: "[I pray] that He would grant you, according to the riches of His glory, to be strength-ened with power through His Spirit in the inner man; so that Christ may dwell in your hearts through faith; and that you, being rooted and grounded in love, may be able to comprehend with all the saints what is the breadth and length and height and depth, and to know the love of Christ which sur-passes knowledge, that you may be filled up to all the fulness of God" (3:16–19, NAS).

David tells us that in God's presence there is "full-ness of joy" and in His right hand are "pleasures forevermore" (Ps. 16:11). I began to move beyond the affirmation of this truth to the tangible, experiential enjoyment of it. It suddenly dawned on me that, whereas I had trusted God with my mind, confident that He was sufficiently sovereign to protect my theology, I had not trusted Him with my emotions.

I still sing about God. I always will. But there's something different in singing *to* God. Yes, I still join with others and sing, "We love Him." But I much prefer engaging God one on one, my heart touching His, and singing, "I love You!"

I soon made a discovery about worship that I believe is found repeatedly in Scripture. Unfortunately, although I read it, I never experienced the reality of it. I'm referring to the outpouring of divine power during times of praise. When God's people exalt and enjoy Him, He releases His power to heal them, to encourage them and to enlighten them, among other things, in a way that is somewhat unique. When God's people worship, He goes to war on their behalf (2 Chron. 20). When God's people worship, He enthrones Himself in their midst (Ps. 22). When God's people worship, He speaks to them and guides them (Acts 13). When God's people worship, He delivers them from their troubles (Acts 16).

Our first healing

I also began obeying the Scriptures concerning my responsibility to pray for the sick. It wasn't a question of who or how many did or did not get healed. It was a question of whether or not we were going to be obedient. I embraced the perspective of John

Wimber, who once said, "I would rather pray for a hundred people and see only one get healed than to pray for none and none get healed." In other words, I finally reached a point at which I refused to allow the fear of failure to justify my disobedience to the Word.

I don't recall the date, but I will never forget the Sunday when a young couple came to me before the service and asked that the elders of the church anoint their infant son and pray for his healing. We were unskilled, but committed to do what James 5 said to do. After the service we gathered in the back room, and I anointed the young boy with oil. I can't give you the precise medical name for his condition, but at six months of age he had a serious liver disorder that would require immediate surgery, possibly even a transplant, if something did not change.

As we prayed, something very unusual happened. It has only happened to me this one time. As we laid hands on him and prayed, I found myself suddenly filled with an overwhelming and inescapable confidence that he would be healed. It was altogether unexpected. I recall actually trying to doubt, but couldn't! I was filled with a faith unshakeable and undeniable. "God," I prayed silently, "You really are going to heal him." I prayed confidently. The family left the room unsure. But not me. I was absolutely certain God had healed him. The next morning the doctor agreed. That little boy was totally healed and is a healthy, happy seven-year-old today.

My visit to the Vineyard

I first met Jack Deere in 1973 while we were students together at Dallas Theological Seminary.

Both of us were strict cessationists. Neither of us would ever have envisioned the theological path that we would one day walk. Jack has told his own story in his book *Surprised by the Power of the Spirit* (Zondervan). After our graduation from seminary we saw little of each other until one day in 1987 when I bumped into Jack on the campus at Dallas. He shared with me some of what God had been doing in his life. Not long after our conversation, he was dismissed from the faculty and eventually joined the staff of the Vineyard Christian Fellowship in Anaheim, California, where John Wimber was serving as senior pastor. Jack and I maintained close contact with each other as he helped and encouraged me in my own pilgrimage.

Jack invited me to attend a large Vineyard conference to be held in Anaheim in January of 1991. I will never forget how I felt as I walked into the Anaheim Convention Center and joined five thousand other believers in worship. Several things happened that week that forever changed my life.

On the second day of the conference I had the opportunity to observe several men pray and minister prophetically to people in one of the smaller rooms at the back of the convention center. After about two hours, my turn came. I sat down across from a man whom I had never met. I was later to learn that he was one of the famous (infamous?) "Kansas City prophets."

This man looked at my name tag, peered deeply into my eyes and proceeded to tell me precisely what I had been praying while alone in my hotel room all week! People in the Vineyard commonly refer to this phenomenon by saying, "He read my mail!" I hadn't told Jack or anyone about my prayer. I had only told God. But evidently God had told this prophetically gifted man! He didn't speak in general or broad terms, but recited to me the very words that I had repeatedly cried out to the Lord the previous three nights. I was tempted to search my hotel room for a bugging device, but there was no need. I had just had my first experience with what I now know as New Testament prophetic ministry. True to Scripture, I was profoundly encouraged, consoled and exhorted (1 Cor. 14:3).

This was my first experience with one of the miraculous gifts of the Holy Spirit. I believed in the gift of prophecy before I ever went to Anaheim. I had just never seen it in operation. Since that day in January of 1991 I have witnessed countless instances of prophetic utterance and, by God's grace, have even been used of the Lord on a few occasions to speak similarly into the lives of other people. Let me briefly share one of those instances.

A strange word

In the fall of 1994 a young couple from out of town attended one of the weekend seminars conducted by the Grace Training Center, the full-time Bible school at Metro Christian Fellowship, which I now serve as president. I knew nothing about them, other than that they were acquaintances of friends of ours in Oklahoma City. I met them for the first time on Saturday of the seminar, and invited them to join several other people who would be coming to our home for fellowship and worship later that evening.

There were about thirty people crammed into our

living room that night as we sang and prayed and enjoyed the presence of the Lord. About fifteen minutes into worship, something unusual happened to me. Without warning, the word *endometriosis* sprang into my mind. *You* think it sounds strange! You should have been in my shoes! Absolutely nothing had been said to trigger that word in my mind. Absolutely nothing had been done to incline me to think along those lines. I'm not the sort of guy who sits around and casually meditates on the subject of endometriosis!

I was a bit perplexed by it, but the impression was so strong that I simply asked the Lord to help me understand why and for whom the word had come. Immediately He directed my attention to the visiting couple. "She's the one," I sensed the Lord saying. I was in something of a pickle. That particular subject is very personal and not the sort of thing you bring up in a crowd of thirty people. It has the potential to be both embarrassing and hurtful. I tried to put it out of my mind altogether and focus again on the worship that was continuing among the others present.

But the Lord wouldn't let me. Finally, I got up and quietly went back to my bedroom. I took one of my business cards and wrote the young lady's name on it along with the word *endometriosis.* I returned to the living room and took my seat. After worship ended, I tentatively said, "I want to be careful and sensitive about this, but I believe God has given me a word for someone here. The last thing I want to do is embarrass anyone, so I'm not asking you to identify yourself. In fact, I think I know who it is. But I'll leave it up to you whether or not you want to say so. I think the Lord has told me that a lady here has endometriosis."

No sooner had the words come out of my mouth than the lady whom I suspected thrust her hand into the air and said, "That's for me!" I told her that, indeed, I thought she was the one. I then took the card from my pocket and gave it to her. She was overwhelmed. But more important, she was profoundly encouraged and consoled. I told her that I didn't know if God had given me this word because He wanted to heal her. I certainly wasn't about to make any promises that God Himself hadn't made. Perhaps He revealed this to me simply to tell her in a powerfully undeniable way, "Yes, I know who you are and where you are. I know about your condition. I have indeed heard your prayers and your cries." If that alone was God's purpose, it worked. We proceeded to pray for her, asking the Lord to heal her and to bless her and her husband with the children for which they had been praying for several years. She left with renewed faith, renewed confidence, renewed hope and "joy inexpressible and full of glory" (1 Pet. 1:8). She later gave birth to twins!

Hooked!

My time in Anaheim at the Vineyard Conference was incredible. As I flew back to Oklahoma, I wrote down three things that impressed me about the people at the conference. These are by no means the only things characteristic of their Christian walk. I only want to mention what I saw, heard and sensed that created in my heart a cry: "Lord, I want that!"

1. These people had an unashamed, extravagant affection for Jesus.

I love Jesus. I have loved Jesus ever since I was a child. But I can't say that my love for Jesus had been unashamed or extravagant. I had always been careful to keep my love for Jesus private and under control. When in public I was diligent to express my affection for Christ only in ways that conformed with accepted religious traditions. I was careful not to embarrass myself or make other people feel uncomfortable with my devotion to the Son of God. But these people were open, honest, passionate, carefree and proud of their affection and love for the Son of God. I saw it. I heard it. I wanted it.

2. These people manifested a sense of immediacy in their relationship with God.

I don't know a better term to use than *immediacy*. By it I mean a sense of God's proximity, His nearness, what theologians call His *immanence*. They lived, talked, laughed and sang as if God were right there in and with them. Their God was not a distant deity or a remote ruler. To use the words of an old hymn, He "walked with them and talked with them and told them they were His own." I believed God was near. But I rarely sensed it. I rarely lived as if it were true. I had become an evangelical deist, one who worshiped a God far off, removed from the daily struggles of life. But not these people. Once again, I saw it. I heard it. And once again, I wanted it.

3. These people prayed anywhere, at any
   time, for anyone, for any reason.

I was standing in line for a hot dog during the
break, eavesdropping on the prayers of the people
in front of me. They stopped right there in line, laid
hands on a needy friend and prayed! None of this
"I'll pray for you!" as a Christian way of saying
"Good-bye. Have a nice day!" They didn't say it.
They didn't even promise it. They did it. Why?
Because they had the spiritual audacity actually to
believe God's Word. They really believed God listened to them. They really believed God would
answer them. They took seriously a verse that I had
only memorized but failed to practice: "You do not
have because you do not ask" (James 4:2, NAS). I saw
it. I heard it, and yes, I wanted it.

My introduction to Paul Cain

I first became aware of Paul Cain's ministry in
1991 and finally met him in March of 1993 at a conference in Houston, Texas. Paul is one of the
gentlest, most humble and unassuming people I
know. Paul has played an incalculable role in the
prophetic history of our church, so I'll have more to
say about him and his life a bit later.

On the last night of this conference, Paul called
me out of the audience and delivered a ten-minute
prophetic word of encouragement. The text he used
was from Isaiah 58. In the course of his message,
throughout which he had been speaking of my ministry and how God wanted to use me, he paused. He
said, "Sam, I know you have thought, *Who's going to*

30

take care of me? If I give my life to pastoral ministry, if I deny myself and take up my cross, who will watch over me? Sam, the Lord says to you, 'I will guide you personally. I will guide you personally; I will take care of you. I will guide thee continually.'" This very pointed application of the first phrase in Isaiah 58:11 was then followed by Paul's quoting the rest of the verse: "...and satisfy your desire in scorched places, and give strength to your bones; and you will be like a watered garden, and like a spring of water whose waters do not fail" (NAS).

At the time, I didn't fully appreciate Paul's words. I thought they were nice, but I couldn't make much sense of the application. After all, this was March of 1993. I was committed to the ministry in Ardmore. I had no intention of leaving. Our family was happy, and the church was prospering. Joining a Vineyard church was the farthest thing from my mind. Immediately after the meeting, Jack Deere came to me and said, "Sam, you may not understand fully what Paul said, but get a videotape of it and write it down. It will probably take on new meaning in a few months."

As it turned out, Jack's advice was right on target. Moving day was August 18, 1993. It was one of the most difficult and depressing days of my life. We had spent the day before helping the movers load our belongings and saying good-bye to family and friends. We were scheduled to meet the movers at our new residence in Kansas City at 12:00 noon. It was very early Wednesday morning, August 18. I was depressed and worried that I had made a terrible mistake. I was fearful of the new responsibilities, both financial and occupational, that I was to assume upon our arrival in Kansas City. Ann was tired and depressed. Our daughters were just tired.

Melanie was in the car with me. Ann and Joanna were in the minivan. As Melanie rubbed the sleep from her eyes, she opened a going-away gift she had received from the principal of her school. It was one of those verse-a-day calendars that people set on their kitchen counters or on their bed-stand. I said, "Well, Melanie, this is as big a day as we've ever had. We're moving to Kansas City. What's our verse for today?" She opened the calendar and turned to August 18. If you haven't figured it out yet, the verse for that day was . . . Isaiah 58:11! This was the precise verse the Lord had given Paul Cain as a special promise to me four months earlier. (By the way, I tore out that page of the calendar and carry it with me as a daily reminder of God's faithfulness. If we should ever meet, ask me and I'll be happy to show it to you.)

It was as if I had been hit with a bolt of lightning. I slammed on the breaks, jumped out of the car and ran back to Ann, who was probably thinking that I had changed my mind about the move. I shouted, "Ann, you'll never guess what has happened! Today is the day. We're moving. We're stepping out in faith. And look at what verse is for today!"

Someone told me there are approximately thirty thousand verses in the Bible. There are three hundred sixty-five days in the year. You tell me: What are the odds of that one verse appearing on that one day? They are astronomical, no doubt. But to a God who controls the universe and speaks through His people whom He has gifted prophetically, it is a mere trifle. To me, it was stunning, supernatural confirmation that indeed we had heard the Lord correctly and were doing His will.

The conference and the call

Needless to say, the first six months of 1993 were filled with events that to this day leave me breathless. Little did we know that June of that year would be the most astounding time of all.

In April, while I was attending my first weekend seminar at Metro Vineyard Fellowship (now Metro Christian Fellowship) in Kansas City, Mike Bickle suggested that I consider joining the staff as president of Grace Training Center. I was surprised by his invitation. He said that he wanted Ann and me to return for the summer conference in June so that he could make the offer official to both of us. When I told Ann what Mike had said, she sensed that perhaps in the distant future it might come about, but not anytime soon.

We returned to Kansas City for the June conference. It began on Tuesday night. On Wednesday morning Mike did indeed issue a formal invitation, saying, "I know you're the man for the job. You can have it in three weeks or three years. I'll wait." Ann thought it might be three years. She was wrong.

On Wednesday night, Ann's life was forever changed. So, too, was our marriage. Mike was scheduled to preach part two of a message he had begun the previous evening. Five minutes into his message he stopped and said, "I can't do this. God has something else in mind. I want the worship team to come back up on stage, and let's wait and see what God has for us." There were two thousand people in attendance, but it was as if what God had in store next was for Ann in particular.

Mike and one of the prophetic ministers both discerned that the Lord wanted to set free those in the audience who were oppressed by and in bondage to a spirit that evoked the fear of failing God. They asked for anyone to stand who wanted healing and deliverance from a spirit of failure and the shame it brings. Ann instantly stood to her feet, as did several others. Yes, I was surprised. I asked myself, "Why is she standing?" I was actually a little embarrassed.

As the worship team sang, two ladies whom neither Ann nor I had ever seen before or since laid hands on her and began singing in tongues. What I saw happening before my eyes was the spiritual transformation of my wife of twenty-eight years. Intense sensations began in her temples and then gradually coursed throughout her body. She struggled to remain standing as the ladies lovingly continued their ministry to her. At one point, Ann reached up and patted their hands and said, "I'm OK. That's enough," all the while saying to herself, "But I'm a pastor's wife. I'm supposed to be OK." Thank God, the ladies knew better. "No," they said, "let's stay with this a while longer and see what God will do."

Ann and I have been married twenty-eight years. We've had a really good marriage. We love and respect each other. God has blessed us with two wonderful children. But in our third year of marriage, which was my second year of seminary, I deeply wounded my wife. No, I have always been faithful. It wasn't immorality. But in my insensitivity and selfishness I had deeply hurt her. To make it worse, I was too naive to recognize what I'd done. Ann never told me. But from that day on, until that night in June in Kansas City in 1993, Ann had shut both God and me out of a part of her life.

She loved God. She served Him faithfully. But there was a part of her soul, deep down, hidden and carefully guarded, that she kept for herself. She loved me, too. She had been a wonderfully faithful wife and mother. But there was a part of her that didn't trust either one of us. In her bitterness and fearful self-protective reaction to my sin against her, she had opened the door to the enemy. As she describes it, "I had let the sun go down on my anger and thereby gave the enemy a foothold" (Eph. 4:26–27).

She said she had made an inner vow never again to be that vulnerable to God or me. Truly, the enemy used this opportunity to gain a stronghold in her life that could only be overcome by the power of the Holy Spirit. Virtually every day for seventeen years, she listened to the voice in her head that said, "Sam hasn't made you happy. God hasn't made you happy. Come with me. I will make you happy."

For all those many years Ann lived with what she calls a hole in her soul filled with black goo. It crippled her relationship with the Lord. It adversely affected her intimacy with me. It daily tormented her with guilt, frustration and shame. At night she often had dreams that left her feeling dirty. She blamed herself for being such a failure as a Christian that those kinds of dreams would invade her soul. Ann never revealed her struggles to me for all those years because of the shame she felt.

As the ladies prayed and sang in the Spirit over Ann, the cleansing power of the Holy Spirit was released in her body and the black goo came out. I know it sounds strange, but that's the only way Ann knows how to explain it. The ugly mass began to explode upward from her toes through her heart and out her mouth. Her tears flowed as she was carried into a new revelation of Christ's love for her. The deep dark hole was suddenly filled with the light of forgiveness, freedom and cleanness.

The next day as Ann and I were heading to the airport in the car, she suddenly grasped her head with her hands and exclaimed, "It's gone! It's gone!"

"What's gone?" I asked.

"The voice is gone," she said. "The voice that I've heard and fought against every day for years is gone!" What a change it has made. Our marriage isn't perfect, but it's great. Our relationship, spiritually and physically, is now on an entirely different plane. Yes, we do believe it was a demonic being, a tormenting spirit that oppressed Ann for all those many years. We aren't ashamed to talk about deliverance. Oh, what a glorious word! Set free by the mercy and cleansing grace of Jesus! Praise God! I got a new wife. Together we got a new marriage! Don't hesitate to ask her. She'd love nothing more than to tell you all about it.

That's only the beginning. Wednesday night, after her deliverance, Ann had a spiritual dream. She found herself scaling a high concrete wall that she knew in the dream represented our move to Kansas City. Melanie was on the wall with her, as was Joanna. But when she looked for me, I was still on the ground. My body was wrapped with bands that pinned my arms to my side and prevented me from doing anything but hopping up and down. She knew instinctively that it symbolized the struggle that I, more than anyone else, would have in making the move.

On Friday of that same week, I had the opportunity to receive ministry from several prophetically gifted people. None of us knew each other. The first to speak was a man named Phil Elston. He looked at me and said, "Your father is not living. He died several years ago and is now with the Lord. Your relationship with him was very special. Your love and respect for him were unusually deep and personal. In fact, since his death you have tried hard to carry on his reputation. He was an honorable man, and you are proud to be known as his son." I can't begin to tell you how accurate that word was. Phil shared a few other things about my relationship with my dad, all of which were remarkably on target.

Next a young lady with a Canadian accent spoke to me. I later learned that it was Anita Ruis, wife of David Ruis, whose worship ministry had very recently impacted Ann very powerfully. Anita said, "I just had a vision of you. You were wrapped from head to toe with bands, holding your arms at your side. All you could do was hop up and down. But then I saw this huge pair of scissors suddenly snip the bands and set you free." Wow! How could she know what Ann had dreamed about me only two days earlier? Well, I know how. What do you think?

That very night Paul Cain arrived in town. Mike Bickle and I were very careful to make certain that Paul knew nothing of Mike's invitation that I become president of Grace Training Center. We both wanted an independent confirmation of what we felt was the leading of the Lord. I wondered how God would provide the needed confirmation.

Toward the conclusion of Paul's time of prophetic ministry, he asked me to stand up. He said, "Sam, God spoke to me very clearly about you being trained for training. Promotion comes from the Lord, and it looks like it is coming from the north. And yes, you will be moving soon." Grace Training Center in Kansas City was very much in my heart before Paul ever spoke. In fact, I had already made the decision to move. Paul's word was a welcome confirmation to both Mike and me.

Angels!

Those first few months in Kansas City were incredibly difficult. Ann's dream, which indicated that I would have a particularly hard time of it, was all too painfully true. I knew we were supposed to be at Metro Vineyard. I never doubted the clarity of God's call. In those days I would often rehearse in my mind the events that I've been sharing with you. Each time I was encouraged. But it still hurt to leave family and friends in Ardmore. My affection for the people at Christ Community Church was deep and remains so to this day. I experienced a lot of guilt, feeling as if I had abandoned them in a time of special need. I needed encouragement. I got it.

I'm not suggesting that what I'm about to describe is normative for every believer. All I know is what God graciously did for Ann and me in a time of desperation.

One night in early November 1993, I had gone to bed about 11 P.M. I'm an especially sound sleeper—virtually nothing can wake me up. Ann had fallen asleep in Joanna's room after having put her to bed. About 1 A.M., Ann entered our bedroom. There above the headboard, as she describes it, was the outline of what looked like an angel. Since Ann had never seen an angel before, she quickly dismissed the possibility and got in bed.

You must understand, of course, that I only know this because she later told me. I was sound asleep. But I was dreaming. In my dream I distinctly heard four chimes. The sound was clear and pristine. The experience was so profound that, uncharacteristically, I woke up. Just as I was coming out of my sleep, I felt Ann's fingernails digging into my arm. "Did you hear the chimes?" she asked in a quivering voice.

"Yeah. But how could you hear what I was dreaming?" By this time we were both wide awake!

The idea that Ann had heard with her physical ears what I heard only in my mind was enough to bring me completely out of my slumber. I immediately said, "Did the chimes sound like this...?" at which point I quietly repeated for her the brief melody. Her fingernails dug even deeper into my flesh.

"Yes! What do we do now?"

Being the theologian that I am, I said, "I don't know. What do you think?"

"I think we ought to pray," she responded with great profundity. We did. Later Ann told me that the chimes sounded as if they were coming from over by the door to our bedroom, some fifteen feet away. As for me, they were in my head.

A few days later, indeed the night before I was to leave to speak at a conference in Dallas, we had another incident in our bedroom. On several occasions during the week preceding my departure, a number of people had prayed for me. They had especially asked that God would send angelic protection, provision and encouragement. (See Psalm 91:11–13; Matthew 4:11; Hebrews 1:14.)

What happened next was, in my opinion, God's answer to their prayers on my behalf. I was again awakened by Ann's breathless voice. "Is that Lucy?" Lucy is our cat.

"No. I locked Lucy in the garage. Go to sleep."

A few moments later Ann again whispered, "Do you hear the footsteps?" They were on my side of the bed, soft but distinct. Lucy really was in the garage. But someone was in our room.

What were the chimes? Who made the footsteps? Skeptics will try to dismiss it all as just so much hyperspirituality. I can't do anything about that. I can only tell you in the integrity of my heart what we experienced. You have to make up your own mind. Ann and I are convinced beyond doubt that in the case of both the chimes and footsteps we were the recipients of two separate angelic visitations. In both cases, no words were spoken, but the room and our hearts were filled with awe and fear and an increased awareness of God's presence and power.

A few months later, Ann was still wondering why it all happened. So she asked the Lord. His answer was simple and to the point: "To give you courage." Of course! If we needed anything at that time it was the courage to persevere, the courage to press on, the courage to hold fast to what we knew was God's leading in our move to Kansas City.

We don't live each day with the expectation of an angelic visitation. We don't make our decisions based on supernatural experiences like the ones I've described. We look first and fundamentally to the written Word of God. But we do bow before the God of heaven and earth and say, "Thank You. We love You. We praise You for these tokens of Your presence and the encouragement they bring."

Sam and his precious family stand before us, along with many others, both highly educated and not, as credible witnesses that God does indeed communicate directly by His Spirit to people today. Cessationism will cease before it's all said and done—I believe that God Himself will see to it.

<h3 style="text-align:center">THE APOSTOLIC EXPECTATION FOR THE
CONTINUANCE OF THE SIGN GIFTS</h3>

I believe that the following Scripture passage validates that it was the clear expectation of the first apostles of Jesus that the supernatural gifts of the Spirit would continue to operate in the church until the personal return of Jesus to this earth.

> I thank my God always concerning you for the grace of God which was given to you by Christ Jesus, that you were enriched in everything by Him in all utterance and all knowledge, even as the testimony of Christ was confirmed in you, so that you come short in no gift, eagerly waiting for the revelation of our

Lord Jesus Christ, who will also confirm you to the end, that you may be blameless in the day of our Lord Jesus Christ.

—1 CORINTHIANS 1:4–8

The "all utterance and all knowledge" that enriched the Corinthians and confirmed them in the Christian faith is an obvious reference to the supernatural manifestations and gifts of the Spirit upon which Paul elaborates in chapters 12–14. Verse 7 validates the fact that Paul had the charismatic gifts in view. Without a doubt, he expected these gifts of God's grace to continue their "confirming" work in the body of Christ to the very end— "the revelation of our Lord Jesus Christ" and "the day of our Lord Jesus Christ."

Chapter 2

THE GOD WHO SPEAKS

T HERE ARE TWO things (among many others) about God that I find to be equally amazing: He is a God who *hides* Himself, and He is a God who *reveals* Himself. He has been known to be extremely effective at both of these contrasting abilities! In Isaiah, God refers to both of these activities in the same text of Scripture:

> Truly You are God, who hide Yourself, O God of Israel, the Savior!...I have not spoken in secret, in a dark place of the earth; I did not say to the seed of Jacob, "Seek Me in vain"; I, the LORD, speak right-eousness, I declare things that are right.
>
> —ISAIAH 45:15, 19

God calls us to seek after Him. We are not called do this because He is *lost!* We are called to do this because He is *hiding,* and He wants us to know the spiritual thrill of seeking after Him and then finding Him.

> For I know the thoughts that I think toward you,
> says the LORD, thoughts of peace and not of evil, to
> give you a future and a hope. Then you will call
> upon Me and go and pray to Me, and I will listen to
> you. And you will seek Me and find Me, when you
> search for Me with all your heart. I will be found by
> you, says the LORD.
>
> —JEREMIAH 29:11–14

This dynamic between our heavenly Father and us is really not so strange, for we often see a similar relational dynamic played out between parents and their children. "Peekaboo" is one of the first joyous, playful games parents play with their little ones. What do we so enjoy about this little love game? As the parent hides his or her face and then suddenly shows it, the common love bond is rediscovered. Both the parent and the child feel that love all over again as they gaze into one another's faces. The hiding creates a tension through the deliberate distancing of the beloved. The temporary hiding also hinders the taking for granted of the love bond between the two. When the one hiding appears again, the thrill of joyous reunion and intimacy rushes in to ease the tension created by the hiding.

When children grow up a little more, the hiding becomes more sophisticated, and the seeking becomes more intense through the game of "hide-and-seek." There is a unique thrill that is very basic to the dynamic of one hiding well and the other discovering the hiding place and the loved one hiding there. When a child cannot find the parent, after a time she or he will begin to panic and cry out. The parent may give hints as to where he or she can be found. The parent often allows himself or herself to be found. In this way, the discovery skills of the child are honed, and courage is developed.

Why are these little games so universal to the human experience? I believe they are pictures of a dynamic in our relationship with our Creator. It could be said that God has chosen to play hide-and-seek with humanity. However, this is not a game or a cruel joke of some kind. Rather, this dynamic flows out of His passionate love for us. God does not need anything, but He wants to be wanted and sought out. God knows how awesome He is, and He experiences no shame or false humility about it! He knows that He is most worthy to be sought after and found. He knows the delight, satisfaction and love we will encounter when we connect with Him.

God, who is a society of love within His trinitarian self, wants to export His well-being to all creation. Therefore, God has ordained that we should seek Him as the primary purpose, meaning and reason of our existence. He has said that if we do, then all other things in life will take their proper place.

> But seek first the kingdom of God and His right-eousness, and all these things shall be added to you.
> —MATTHEW 6:33

Have you happened to notice that God is invisible to us in this age? If nothing else spoke of how He is playing hide-and-seek with us, this by itself should convince us that He is. God could so easily absolutely "prove" His existence to humanity. Yet, He has chosen not to do so. He has certainly left us many convincing hints of His presence in this universe. He desires a relationship with those who care to follow these signs along the trail to discover His reality. God is desirous of voluntary, not coerced, love. Forced love is no love at all.

The Invisible God Nearby

In the following passage, the apostle Paul was addressing the philosophers in Athens.

> God, who made the world and everything in it, since He is Lord of heaven and earth, does not dwell in temples made with hands. Nor is He worshiped with men's hands, as though He needed anything, since He gives to all life, breath, and all things. And He has made from one blood every nation of men to dwell on all the face of the earth, and has determined their preappointed times and the boundaries of their dwellings, so that they should seek the Lord, in the hope that they might grope for Him and find Him, though He is not far from each one of us; for in Him we live and move and have our being, as also some of your own poets have said, "For we are also His offspring."
>
> —Acts 17:24–28

I so love this passage of scripture. Paul presents God as the grand genius of the universe. He is the *master scientist* who has created all things both visible and invisible. (Humanity has yet to discover the exact nature of the relationship between matter and spirit.) God is the designer and owner of the universe, and He is transcendent and absolutely self-sufficient. We do not need to provide for Him—He is the one who has provided for us. He is not "worshiped with men's hands, as though He needed anything," but He is to be worshiped by men's hearts because He wants something. Specifically, He *wants to be wanted* by us.

Paul then presents God as the *master of all human history*. God made from one person (a reference to Adam) all the nations of humanity that have lived on the face of the earth. Moreover, God is also the *master of geopolitics*. He has personally preappointed their "times" and the "boundaries of their habitation." Imagine all the agony and ecstasy bound up in this simple statement. God has overseen the rising and falling of the nations throughout history. Whenever He has determined for their geographic boundaries to *move*—even a little—many have wept, many have lost, many have died, many have rejoiced, many have gained and many have been spared.

Paul says that God has done all this for one primary reason: that humanity should "seek the Lord." This is the essence of the very purpose for our lives. This is why we are on the planet at all. This is what brings meaning and dignity into the human soul. It is found in our seeking after the invisible God. The apostle goes on to say that God actually has a hope in His heart that we will "grope for Him and find Him, though He is not far from each one of us." This could be called the "hope to grope." God has ordained the struggle, because He wants to be wanted by us. And, when we do want Him, it honors Him and brings pleasure to His heart.

Even though God doesn't "need" anything, there is something we can "give" Him! We can give Him our attention and our love. And He will receive it. The journey is meaningful, and the destination can be reached. The invisible God is not far from any one of us—He can and wills to be found by us. He is *transcendent,* but He is also *immanent*—He is nearby, concerned, involved and accessible to us.

Jesus told us that two sparrows don't fall to the ground without God's intimate knowledge. And then He said that we are more valuable to God than birds. We live, move and have our being by the power of His providence, which upholds the very universe around us. He also periodically performs unusual acts of His power—miracles—in order to remind us that He is indeed behind the ordinary and usual wonders all around us. *Miracles* remind us of *providence* and serve to keep us humble and full of worship at all times and seasons. For this kind of God to communicate to and even through His own creation by prophetic activity is not only feasible, it is reasonable and even to be expected. Why are we so full of doubt?

Indeed, God is a God who hides Himself, but He not only plays *hide-and-seek* with humanity, He also plays *show-and-tell* with us!

> The secret things belong to the LORD our God, but those things which are revealed belong to us and to our children forever, that we may do all the words of this law.
>
> —DEUTERONOMY 29:29

God's willingness to show Himself to His children— and the fact that He is doing so today—is helping to heal the church of her boredom and powerlessness as faith is growing for the supernatural interventions of God in the midst of our earthly life and mission. One of these supernatural gifts of the Holy Spirit is the gift of prophecy. I define *prophecy* simply as "people receiving and/or communicating direct revelation from God through the power of the Holy Spirit." It's amazing that some people, who believe in the existence of God, find it incredible that God could or would do such a thing.

On the other hand, there are millions of people who claim to have heard God speak to them in one way or another. A well-known American female comedian has allegedly said, "Why is it that when we refer to people talking to God, we call it *prayer,* but when we refer to God talking to people we call it *schizophrenia?*" A good question, don't you think? If He really is there, it's not so hard to imagine that He might speak or reveal something to His own creation sometimes, is it?

Upon reflection, the idea that He wouldn't do so seems much more incredible—especially when we consider how full of life, love, wisdom, creativity and purpose God is! Indeed, the Bible makes it abundantly clear that God is a God who speaks and reveals Himself over and over again in many ways.

Prophecy is typically thought of as foretelling the future, and this can be true. The fact that God reveals the future through His prophets is one of the things that He says distinguishes Him from all the other so-called gods of the nations.

> "Present your case," says the LORD. "Set forth your arguments," says Jacob's King. "Bring in your idols to tell us what is going to happen. Tell us what the former things were, so that we may consider them and know their final outcome. Or declare to us the things to come, tell us what the future holds, so we may know that you are gods. Do something,

whether good or bad, so that we will be dismayed
and filled with fear. But you are less than nothing
and your works are utterly worthless; he who
chooses you is detestable."

—ISAIAH 41:21–24, NIV

Hundreds of prophecies were spoken and recorded in
the Scriptures through the prophets of Israel, Jesus Christ
Himself and the New Testament writers that have come
to pass—some with uncanny detail. Fulfilled prophecy is
one, if not the main, evidence for the truth of the Bible
and the claims of Christianity. We would expect God to
give evidences such as this if He expects us to put our
lives on the line for proclaiming the only true way of faith
and salvation to all the people of the world.

However, prophecy is more than foretelling. It is, more
essentially, a *forthtelling* of the mind and truth of God.
Therefore, it can relate to the past and present as well as
to the future. God spoke to Moses and revealed to him
what had happened in the very beginning of time. God
inspired Moses to write it down in the Book of Genesis.
Many times the prophets of God told their listeners what
God was saying in the present tense—not only what He
would do in the future.

The prophetic ministry, in the broadest sense of the
term, includes any supernatural knowledge given to men
by God Himself. I believe that it is important to broaden
our working definition of the prophetic so that we come
to fully appreciate its importance in Christian doctrine and
experience. Throughout this book, when I use the term
prophetic, I am using it as an umbrella term and am referring to more than just the specific gift of prophecy. I am
also including things like supernatural visions, dreams,

visitations, trances and words of knowledge and wisdom. It has to do primarily with the direct inspiration and communication of God toward and through human beings.

The *gospel* is maybe the most *prophetic* thing the earth has ever known. The Jewish prophets foretold it for centuries, and its very message is the power of God unto salvation for every one who believes (Rom. 1:16). Christians, to this day, are called to proclaim the Word of God under the anointing and in the power of the Holy Spirit, humbly and boldly. If we desire to be really *prophetic,* then let us be sure to share the good news of our faith with the many unbelievers all around us.

The Bible is the prophetic book of *Yahweh*—the one true God who has revealed Himself and His power throughout history. The apostle Peter referred to the Bible as "prophecy of Scripture" (2 Pet. 1:20–21).

All of Scripture's words have been directly inspired and superintended by the Holy Spirit as God chose human vessels to pen the words. It is therefore infallible and wholly reliable. It tells the histories of prophetic men and women to whom and through whom God spoke: Abraham, Joseph, Moses, Deborah, Samuel, David, Isaiah, Elijah, Jeremiah, Daniel, Joel, Mary, Peter, John, Paul and a host of others. It records their inspired words and deeds and their interactions with this one true God. God came to us in the Person of Jesus of Nazareth. Jesus was from eternity past God the Son, now made flesh—fully God and fully man: the very Word of God. This title sounds rather prophetic to me.

Jesus Christ was the greatest prophet and the prototype of all other genuine prophetic ministry. He bled and died on a cross as a substitutionary sacrifice for the sins of all people. He is the only Savior and Lord of all. His claims

51

of divinity were proven by His resurrection from the dead. He often confirmed the infallibility and prophetic nature of the Scriptures by His statements about them, as did His chosen apostles. In light of this, all other claims of divine revelation must be measured by and against the content and spirit of the Holy Scriptures. No other revelation from God will contradict properly understood and applied truths of the Bible. Scripture must be laid as a template over all other supposed revelation for evaluation and judgment.

It is also important to point out that even the infallible divine revelation of Scripture has the potential of being *misinterpreted* and *misapplied* by fallible human beings. Indeed, this happens all the time, and it has happened to us all at one time or another. The point is that this dynamic does not invalidate the validity of the revelation that God has given to us though the Scriptures. And, even though they may not be perfectly understood by us, they are monumentally useful to us nonetheless. Please don't throw your Bible away simply because you might misunderstand it! Many people write off the value and usefulness of present-day prophetic ministry because it can be misinterpreted and misapplied. Although it is even more easily misunderstood than the Scriptures, and its level of inspiration is not as sure, don't quickly conclude that the Spirit of God isn't moving within the church by this means. You may be surprised to discover how valid and useful it really can be when it is placed in its proper biblical framework.

THE NEED FOR SUBJECTIVE GUIDANCE

Many people assume that since God has given us an infallible record of divine revelation in the Bible, there is therefore no more need for divine communications to human beings. They have invented a teaching that basically implies that our Creator and Lord has muzzled Himself and that He no longer wishes to or will speak directly to people. This is an incredible leap of logic. In their zeal to uphold the supreme value of the Bible, they have silenced God. What a tragedy. What a shame. In fact, God is forever free to do as He pleases. He only will not contradict Himself, for He cannot lie.

There are many issues we face in the course of life that no particular scriptures address. We therefore often stand in need of more subjective guidance from God. The Bible validates this fact over and over again. Yet, we do not have to drown in a sea of subjectivity as we open ourselves to such guidance. We study, meditate upon and diligently apply the teachings of Scripture and then, upon this foundation, we embrace a biblical method of seeking for and testing subjective forms of receiving direction and revelation from God.

I had a remarkable experience in 1985 that illustrates this principle of subjective supernatural guidance. When my wife, Terri, and I were considering relocating from Arkansas (a southern state in the United States) to Michigan (a northern state in the United States) we decided to take a trip to the Detroit area to "spy out the land." We were actually speaking to one another about how it seemed right to both of us that we would move to Detroit and continue our ministry there in my hometown area, even though we had not yet been issued an invitation by anyone there. Through the years, as we traveled to visit my family during vacation times, we made friends with some ministers and churches in that area of the country.

We loaded up our minivan and our three children

(we've since had two more), and then we headed down the road in Little Rock to get on the interstate that would eventually take us to Michigan after over twenty hours of driving. We were only minutes away from our home in Little Rock when a large semitruck passed us on the road and then cut over in front of us so that virtually all we could see was the back end of this very dirty truck. To our utter astonishment, written in dirt across the back of the truck in letters about twelve inches tall were the words, "SAY YES TO DETROIT." Our jaws opened in amazement, and we could only wonder if there was an angel with a dirty finger flying nearby!

We needed that confirmation to our decision to secure our hearts in the will of God. Later we encountered some significant resistance to moving in this direction. The more I have pondered this event, the more profound it has become to me.

THE NECESSITY OF PERSONAL DIVINE REVELATION

The fact is that no one can even become a true Christian without receiving a direct personal revelation from the Holy Spirit. In other words, no one comes to Jesus to be saved without "hearing" from God. In this most basic sense, all Christians have experienced a form of prophecy.

> Most assuredly, I say to you, the hour is coming, and now is, when the dead will hear the voice of the Son of God; and those who hear will live.
>
> —JOHN 5:25

> It is written in the prophets, "And they shall all be taught by God." Therefore everyone who has heard and learned from the Father comes to Me.
> —JOHN 6:45

The prophetic is basic to genuine Christianity simply because it relates to the Word of God being made alive in people's experiences.

> For the word of God is living and powerful, and sharper than any two-edged sword, piercing even to the division of soul and spirit, and of joints and marrow, and is a discerner of the thoughts and intents of the heart.
> —HEBREWS 4:12

God is a prophetic God. The Bible is a prophetic book. Jesus is a prophetic Savior and Lord. Our spiritual fathers and mothers were prophetic. The gospel is prophetic. The church is prophetic in nature and in mission. And divine prophetic purposes are unfolding in our world in our generation. According to the ancient prophecy of Joel 2, we can expect that more people will be ushered into prophetic ministry and experience as the End Times come upon the earth.

MY SUPERNATURAL CONVICTION EXPERIENCE

My first encounter with the voice of God occurred before I was a Christian. It was 1971, and I was sixteen years old. I had, up to that time, only been *superficially exposed* to *superficial Christianity*—that's doubly superficial! I could have been described as a "pseudo-intellectual hippie jock."

OK, I admit that it's a rather odd combination! My older brother, Mark, came into our home one night when I was doing some homework at the dining room table, and he was sopping wet from head to foot. I looked up at him and laughingly asked, "What happened to you?"

Without hesitation he boldly declared, "I got baptized tonight. I got saved. I accepted Jesus Christ as my personal Savior." I was actually offended at this language, thinking that he was somehow viewing Jesus as his "personal Savior" just as a wealthy person might have a "personal chauffeur." I wondered how he "measured up" to having a *personal* Savior. I had never in my whole life heard language like this—"saved," "personal Savior." Furthermore, I knew that no one could get that wet by being sprinkled with a little water!

He then told me that these people at this church had dunked him in a tank of water. It all seemed so strange to me. That night I determined to become a watchdog over his new "religious trip." I would be there to point out all the inconsistencies in his life.

He challenged me to come to church with him, and I decided to go just to prove to him and myself that I would not be so easily manipulated by religious people as he had been.

Attending this service was a true culture shock for me. First of all, every person seemed to be carrying a Bible. I wondered what they each would do with one. One big Bible on the podium would suffice for a church service, wouldn't it? These people also seemed to be pretending that they actually enjoyed being in church. They smiled at each other and gave out hugs and warm handshakes. They seemed actually to know one another. Whenever I had gone to church, it was always something everyone there seemed to *endure* rather than *enjoy.*

When the minister got up to speak, he read a long passage from the Bible and started to discuss what he believed it meant. Nearly everyone in the place read along with him in her or his own Bible, and they nodded their heads approvingly as he talked about the passage. These people were pretending that the Bible was relevant to twentieth-century Americans! I had always considered the Bible to be a book that only people like monks and ancient scribes might partially comprehend. The church service seemed quite weird and yet somewhat entertaining to me.

As the minister continued to preach, I unexpectedly "heard" a voice speak to me. It was not exactly audible, but it might as well have been. It seemed to come from both outside and inside of me. The words I heard shocked me. They went against my belief system. Yet, when I heard them, I instantly knew they were totally true. The voice said, "You have evil inside of you, and if I give you what you deserve, you will go to hell and not heaven."

Now I had always considered myself to be a "good" person. I believed that God existed and that He was a "good" Person, too. Someday I would die and meet Him, and He would accept me because the good within me would outweigh the bad. Then we would get to know each other and have a wonderful eternity together with all the other "good" Americans and probably some "good" people from other less fortunate nations as well. But this voice contradicted my pleasant (and prideful) view of myself. That day I heard (and intellectually understood) for the first time in my life that everyone on the earth needed Jesus Christ to come into a relationship with God the Father. I heard that He died on the cross for our (my) sins and rose again on the third day so that we (I) could be rescued from hell.

I attempted to run away from this experience, denying the reality of what I had heard the voice say to me. Before this experience I had been really enjoying my life—even the sins I had been progressively committing. However, after this encounter with what turned out to be the voice of God, I could no longer enjoy my sinful ways. The Holy Spirit had ruined my sinful life! I knew that there was evil within me and that it wasn't OK. Yet I had no power to reform my attitudes or my behavior. It seemed that I had actually lost some of my ability to resist temptations. As a result, I was becoming internally miserable. I was philosophically opposed to hypocrisy, and yet I had become a hypocrite in my own eyes. For two years I ran from Jesus until He marvelously intervened in my life once again by the voice of the Holy Spirit and called me to Himself.

True prophetic experience has been with humanity from the beginning, and it continues with us to this day. How dare we limit the Holy One of Israel? How dare we suggest that He cannot speak to His own beloved creation? How dare we quickly conclude that someone has been deceived because that person claims that God has spoken directly to or through him or her?

WHY THE CAUTION?

So why is it that the issue of prophecy is fraught with such controversy? The answer is really obvious. Many people throughout history and today have claimed that God has spoken to them about all kinds of things. Yet they have been proven wrong by one means or another. Prophecy receives a bad name through fantasy, foolishness, ignorance, insanity and abuse. Human history is littered with horrendous accounts of people and movements that falsely claimed divine inspiration and communication as their impetus and source of knowledge.

Just a few years ago, a group of apparently well-educated religious people based in California claimed to have heard from God that if they killed themselves, they would be transported to a divine spaceship that followed in the wake of the Hale-Bopp comet as it passed near the earth. To the shock of their loved ones and the whole world, they actually committed mass suicide.

It's understandable that people would be cautious in this very subjective arena of "hearing from God." It is *necessary* that people be cautious in this area! Furthermore, the Bible itself, which affirms the importance and value of true prophecy, confirms this need for caution.

> Beware of false prophets, who come to you in sheep's clothing, but inwardly they are ravenous wolves. You will know them by their fruits.
> —MATTHEW 7:15–16

The consequences of being deceived can be great. What could possibly be more damaging than "speaking for God," having people believe you and then being wrong about it?

On the other hand, what could possibly be more helpful for people than truly hearing from the living God on their behalf? Moses led a whole nation out of slavery into its own land by an extraordinary spirit of prophecy:

> He [God] said, "Listen to my words: When a prophet

of the LORD is among you, I reveal myself to him in visions, I speak to him in dreams. But this is not true of my servant Moses; he is faithful in all my house. With him I speak face to face, clearly and not in riddles; he sees the form of the LORD. Why then were you not afraid to speak against my servant Moses?"
—NUMBERS 12:6–8, NIV

We must embrace the value of, acknowledge the dangers of, face and overcome our fears and quirks regarding the prophetic ministry and learn the practical principles that govern it. Obviously, this ministry will never (and should never) be reduced to an "exact science"—it is subjective by nature. However, it isn't so subjective that no objective parameters exist that safeguard against its abuse.

AN INTERACTIVE RELATIONSHIP WITH GOD

Through his book *In Search of Guidance,* Dallas Willard has done the church a great service. In it, he lays down some excellent philosophical/theological "tracks" for Christians to "run on" pertaining to understanding and evaluating subjective spiritual guidance and prophetic experiences in the light of Scripture and the history of God's interactions with His people. Following is a quote that captures the essence of his approach to this issue.

Preliminary to any successful attempt to understand divine guidance [and I would add, "or the prophetic"—MS] concerns the relationship of our experience to the contents of the Bible and, by extension, to the lives of the saints and heroes of the faith throughout the ages. The humanity of Moses,

60

David and Elijah, and of Paul, Peter and Jesus Christ Himself, of all that wonderful company of riotously human women and men whose experience is recorded in the Bible and in the history of the church, teaches us a very important lesson: Our humanity will not by itself prevent us from knowing and interacting with God as they did. Conversely, if we are really to understand the Bible record itself, we must enter into our study of it on the assumption that the experiences recorded there were basically of the same type as ours would be if we were there. Those who lived through them felt them very much as we would if we were in their place. Unless this feeling of identification comes home to us, the things that happened to the people in the Bible will remain unreal to us.

We will not be able to believe the Bible or find its contents to be really so, because it will have no experiential substance for us. It will mean nothing "concrete," and our blindness will shut the door on those tender overtures of God that now in our own times invite our souls to individual communion with Him (Rev. 3:20). We will be left without the God-provided scriptural keys for interpreting our own encounters with Him and will, like Balaam, be unable to recognize the angel standing directly in our pathway (Num. 22). Failure to read the Bible in this way accounts for two common problems in Christian groups that hold the Bible central to their faith. One is that it becomes simply a book of doctrine, of abstract truth about God, which one can endlessly search without encountering God Himself or hearing His voice. The other problem that arises when we do not understand the experience of biblical characters in terms of our own lives is that we simply stop reading the Bible altogether. Or else we take it "in regular doses," choking it down like medicine because someone told us that it would be good for us, though we really do not find it to be so.

The open secret of many "Bible-believing" churches is that only a very small percentage of their members study the Bible with even the degree of interest, intelligence or joy they bring to bear on their newspaper or *Time* magazine. In my opinion, based on considerable experience, this is primarily because they do not and are not taught how to understand the experience of biblical characters in terms of their own experience.

We must prayerfully but boldly use our God-given imaginations to fill out the reality of the events in terms of what it would be like if we were Moses standing by the bush (Exod. 3:2), little Samuel lying in his darkened room (1 Sam. 3:3–7), Elisha under inspiration from the minstrel (2 Kings 3:15), Ananias receiving his vision about Paul (Acts 9:11) or Peter on his rooftop (Acts 10:10).

We must pray for the faith and for the experiences that would enable us to believe that such things could happen to us. Only so will we be able to recognize them, to accept them and dwell in them when they come.[1]

GOD'S PASSION TO USE HUMAN BEINGS

One of the most amazing truths about God and His kingdom has to be the significant place that He has given to colaboring or partnering with weak, finite and broken human vessels. Yet, the Scriptures declare over and over again that God desires to intimately relate to and use human beings in His service. Moreover, I cannot think of an earthly experience more exhilarating and meaningful to our souls than when we realize that the eternal, infinite and all-powerful God has actually used us for some specific purpose. He really enjoys incorporating us into the accomplishing of His mighty works.

Have you ever gazed up into the heavens on a starry night and felt a sense of your insignificance in this vast universe? My first distinct awareness of God's presence rose up within me when, as an eight-year-old boy, I looked up into the stars one night. I remember feeling how small and powerless I was in this universe. Although I didn't know the word, I pondered "infinity" for the first time in my young life. My little brain hurt just thinking about how the space into which I was looking could not possibly end—there was no ceiling! And if there was one, there had to be something beyond it anyway—even if it was empty space.

Although I was feeling very small at that moment, something very big was taking place in my heart. That evening, I connected with my God-given instinctive knowledge of God, and after that I never really doubted His existence. Paul refers to this internal and instinctive knowledge of God's existence that God has given to every person who has ever been born:

> For since the creation of the world His invisible attributes are clearly seen, being understood by the things that are made, even His eternal power and Godhead, so that they are without excuse.
>
> —ROMANS 1:20

However, it is one thing to know that God exists and to be overwhelmed by the display of His power and yet embrace the truth that God desires personally to interface with us and show His concern for even the details of our lives. The Bible teaches that God is both *transcendent* and *immanent*—above and beyond the creation and yet simultaneously intimately involved with His creation. At eight years old, I could not imagine that God would be concerned with finite human beings. Even so, the Bible teaches from Genesis to Revelation that God indeed is involved with humanity and the created order around us.

In Psalm 8, these two attributes of God's are set side by side. King David declared that he also had his "mind blown" as he considered the majesty of God revealed in the heavenly bodies. Yet, he also understood and embraced God's partnership with humanity—as challenging as it is to understand the reasons behind such an amazing divine arrangement.

> When I consider Your heavens, the work of Your fingers, the moon and the stars, which You have ordained, what is man that You are mindful of him, and the son of man that You visit him? For You have made him a little lower than the angels, and You have crowned him with glory and honor. You have made him to have dominion over the works of Your hands; you have put all things under his feet.
>
> —PSALM 8:3–6

What we, as redeemed humans, really are and have been ordained to do has not yet been fully manifested. Our true identity is "hidden with Christ in God" (Col. 3:3).

In fact, all creation groans and waits to be set free from all the negative effects of the Fall through the full manifestation of God's children (Rom. 8:20–22). We are going to surprise ourselves before it's over!

I love to read the Book of Acts. When I do, I try to "read between the lines" and consider the human emotions and dynamics that surrounded the powerful work of the Holy Spirit. One of my favorite accounts is the conversion of Saul of Tarsus and how God then used a simple "no-name" disciple called Ananias to participate in the greatest miracle of it all.

ANANIAS AND SAUL— GOD LOVES TO USE HUMAN BEINGS

As he journeyed he came near Damascus, and suddenly a light shone around him from heaven. Then he fell to the ground, and heard a voice saying to him, "Saul, Saul, why are you persecuting Me?"

And he said, "Who are You, Lord?"

Then the Lord said, "I am Jesus, whom you are persecuting. It is hard for you to kick against the goads."

So he, trembling and astonished, said, "Lord, what do You want me to do?"

Then the Lord said to him, "Arise and go into the city, and you will be told what you must do."

And the men who journeyed with him stood speechless, hearing a voice but seeing no one. Then Saul arose from the ground, and when his eyes were opened he saw no one. But they led him by the hand and brought him into Damascus. And he was three days without sight, and neither ate nor drank.

Now there was a certain disciple at Damascus

named Ananias; and to him the Lord said in a vision, "Ananias."

And he said, "Here I am, Lord."

So the Lord said to him, "Arise and go to the street called Straight, and inquire at the house of Judas for one called Saul of Tarsus, for behold, he is praying. And in a vision he has seen a man named Ananias coming in and putting his hand on him, so that he might receive his sight."

Then Ananias answered, "Lord, I have heard from many about this man, how much harm he has done to Your saints in Jerusalem. And here he has authority from the chief priests to bind all who call on Your name."

But the Lord said to him, "Go, for he is a chosen vessel of Mine to bear My name before Gentiles, kings, and the children of Israel. For I will show him how many things he must suffer for My name's sake."

—ACTS 9:3–16

My very loose paraphrase goes something like this:

The risen Christ personally confronts a highly intelligent, but angry and unbelieving, Jewish rabbi named Saul on the road one day. A supernatural light suddenly shines upon Saul, and a supernatural voice communicates with him in such a forceful way that he is knocked to the ground. (This is the passage where we get the "doctrine" of Jesus being a "gentleman!") Jesus says to him, "When you mess with my wife, you're messing with me! Cut it out or else. Your arm's too short to box with God."

Scared spitless and shaking uncontrollably, even

before his personal Pentecost, Saul replies, "Lord, are You who I think You are?"

Jesus answers, "You guessed it—I'm Jesus, and I am the Lord! Now go into the city. From now on, our communication will be on a 'need-to-know' basis." The guys with Saul freak out. Come to find out, Jesus struck His precious new believer with blindness—a simple reminder of their little visit. Saul feels led to fast.

The Lord decides that He wants to give some of His weak, but redeemed, human partners a piece of the action. So, Jesus now comes to His friend and servant Ananias in a vision and speaks to him audibly. Ananias, who understands that Jesus often comes to talk to His friends and coworkers in this way, salutes his Captain. Jesus said, "I have an assignment for you. Go and minister to Saul of Tarsus, for he has felt led to spend some time in prayer and fasting. And I know exactly where he is—you know that I always was good at geography. He has actually seen you in a vision—even though I did strike him blind. You know how some people can better see what I am doing when they get their eyes off of this world! Go and heal him, and then he'll probably listen better to what you have to say to him."

Ananias gasps, "Lord, don't You know who this guy is? Haven't You been reading the papers? He hates You and us and…and…and…"

Jesus breaks in and cuts him off, now speaking like a boss with a deadline in mind, "Go! Now!" Of course, Ananias collects himself, goes to Saul and "does the stuff." Jesus made him look real good that day. The end.

This account from the Book of Acts is a "divine appointment" at its best. God is simultaneously working on two ends of the connection between two human parties who are indeed weak, but in whom Christ wants to display His power and grace. He gets the glory, but they get to participate and enjoy the awesome dignity that God confers upon His earthly colaborers. This is the kind of view of God and the variety of working relationship with the divine that will revive the church and bring hope to this world. This is the same sort of "divine appointment" that God wants to arrange for His disciples today. It has always worked this way. This vital and personal relationship with God could be described as "interactive." I believe that entering this quality of prophetically attuned friendship with the Trinity is the only thing that will deliver the body of Christ from the terminal boredom, apathy and irrelevancy from which it has been suffering.

---

1. Dallas Willard, *In Search of Guidance* (San Francisco: Harper Collins, 1993), 25–28.

Chapter 3

BENEFITS OF
THE PROPHETIC

O NE OF THE goals of this book is to help identify
some theological boundaries and practical principles that help to make prophecy more user friendly and
useful in building up the body of Christ. Just as there is a
common body of knowledge that defines *social etiquette*
in any culture, so there is a growing body of knowledge
and experience within the Christian community that is
helping many to discern a *prophetic etiquette.*

If we can discover and embrace such an approach to
prophetic ministry, then we will avoid despising
prophecy and be enabled to get the great good from this
wonderful spiritual gift. However, before we explore the
limits and dangers of prophetic ministry, we need to tout
the blessings of it. If we don't perceive its great value to
the body of Christ, then we will not have the courage or
energy to plow through its difficulties and steward its
challenges.

PROPHECY AND THE CENTRALITY OF CHRIST

> And I fell at his feet to worship him. But he said to me, "See that you do not do that! I am your fellow servant, and of your brethren who have the testimony of Jesus. Worship God! *For the testimony of Jesus is the spirit of prophecy.*"
>
> —REVELATION 19:10, EMPHASIS ADDED

New Testament prophecy is centered in the Person of Jesus Christ. There are two helpful ways to think about the possible meaning of the above verse. First is that the essence or "spirit" of prophecy is the testimony—or the spoken words—*of* the risen Christ Himself *to* His people. Second is that the "testimony"—or the spoken words—*about* Jesus *through* His people is the purpose or "spirit" of prophecy. I believe that both definitions are valid. In either case, prophecy essentially has to do with the unveiling or revealing of the heart, mind and truth of Jesus Christ our Lord. True prophecy will always serve to bring Him glory and honor in the final analysis.

THE PROPHETIC IS BASIC TO NORMAL CHRISTIAN EXPERIENCE

The power of prophecy was not a decorative ornament upon the church of the New Testament. Rather, it was considered to be a basic tool to be utilized in reaching the lost and building believers up in their faith. The Holy Spirit lives and moves within the personality of every believer, and it is only reasonable to assume that He will, from time to time and according to His good pleasure, manifest His personality through His human temples. The lack of supernatural activity in, through and among Spirit-filled Christians would have been, and should be today, considered as subnormal. So often through the centuries believers have lived below the privileges of our high calling as coheirs with Christ of the riches of God's kingdom. The prophetic ministry of the Spirit within the church is one of these honors and blessings.

I think of 1 Corinthians 2 as the most profound and most often overlooked chapter in the New Testament related to the prophetic ministry. It validates how Paul considered prophetic power to be essential and basic to Christian life and ministry. We will look at it in two sections—verses 1–5 and then verses 6–16.

> And I, brethren, when I came to you, did not come with excellence of speech or of wisdom declaring to you the testimony of God. For I determined not to know anything among you except Jesus Christ and Him crucified. I was with you in weakness, in fear, and in much trembling. And my speech and my preaching were not with persuasive words of human wisdom, but in demonstration of the Spirit and of power, that your faith should not be in the wisdom of men but in the power of God.
>
> —1 CORINTHIANS 2:1–5

In these first five verses, Paul describes his primary *evangelistic strategy*. He deliberately chose to focus on the simple and straightforward preaching about the Person of Jesus and the work that He accomplished on the cross in his initial communications with people. His methodology was to preach the "prophetic gospel"—the good news of Jesus Christ foretold in many ways in the

Old Testament. He based his communication of the news about God's New Covenant upon the many fulfilled prophecies of the Old Testaments prophets concerning Messiah *Yeshua*. His method of evangelism focused upon first reasoning with the Jews and then with the Gentiles, and he proved to them from the Scriptures that Jesus was the Christ. If people were going to reject the message of Christianity, Paul wanted to make certain that they stumbled over the plain truth about Christ—God made flesh—coming to die as a substitutionary sacrifice for the sins of all humanity upon the cross and being raised from the dead on the third day by the power of the Holy Spirit in order to open the way of salvation to all peoples. To reject Christianity for some other reason would be a greater and unnecessary tragedy.

> Then Paul, as his custom was, went in to them, and for three Sabbaths reasoned with them from the Scriptures, explaining and demonstrating that the Christ had to suffer and rise again from the dead, and saying, "This Jesus whom I preach to you is the Christ."
>
> —ACTS 17:2–3

In the same tradition of speaking "the word of the Lord" with supernatural power like the Old Testament prophets, but now also combined with New Testament apostolic authority, Paul preached passionately about Christ Jesus to all people. The power of the Holy Spirit worked with him to *confirm* the truth of the message. Elements of prophetic speech and knowledge are often operative in this kind of evangelism. Some have called this method of winning the lost *power evangelism*.

> Therefore they stayed there a long time, speaking boldly in the Lord, who was bearing witness to the word of His grace, granting signs and wonders to be done by their hands.
>
> —Acts 14:3

In Paul's ministry, signs and wonders followed the proclamation of the gospel just as Jesus had promised that they would. Moreover, Paul *relied upon* God's granting these kinds of miracles so that people's faith would not rest upon mere ideas and words, but also upon the clear demonstration of God's supernatural power in their experience. A faith established upon these combined elements would not be easily shaken by the man-made philosophies and religions of this world.

> "And these signs will follow those who believe: In My name they will cast out demons; they will speak with new tongues, they will take up serpents; and if they drink anything deadly, it will by no means hurt them; they will lay hands on the sick, and they will recover."...And they went out and preached everywhere, the Lord working with them and confirming the word through the accompanying signs. Amen.
>
> —Mark 16:17–18, 20

In verses 6–16 of 1 Corinthians 2, Paul describes his primary *edification strategy* for the body of Christ. Once people understood and believed the simple gospel, he would go on and begin to teach them the deeper truths and realities of our faith. After they were established in the basics, he sought to wean them off "milk" and to nourish them with the "meat" of God's Word and ways in

Christ (1 Cor. 3:1–2). The truths about God and His kingdom are inexhaustible in regard to their fascinating and transforming beauty and glory. We are called to continually grow in our experiential knowledge of the Trinity. I believe that this growth dynamic will even continue throughout the ages to come.

It is at this point that the prophetic revelation and ministry, which are given to edify the body of Christ, become extremely important (1 Cor. 14:3). However, when people or movements seek to move into a strong prophetic ministry without keeping the simple gospel at the heart of their message, that expression of the prophetic will become *eccentric* in one way or another.

During the healing movement, which began in the late 1940s in North America, the message that God endorsed with signs, wonders, miracles and strong prophetic anointing was the "message of the cross" (1 Cor. 1:17–18). As these acts of power began to manifest, the positive responses of believers and the negative reactions of critics worked together to subtly pull the anointed God-ordained ministers of the movement into teaching about and defending the *miracles* instead of simply proclaiming the *message* of the cross of Christ. This opened the door for *the flesh* to find expression, and the movement lost its initial purity, giving way to competition, jealousy, envy, greed and moral compromise. God lifted His glory off the movement after a couple of years, although it continued to enjoy a measure of blessing and power.

Since then, I believe that God has been waiting to release this degree of spiritual power to a generation of believers and leaders who will learn from the failures of the past in order to escape the satanic temptations and snares that inevitably appear with the demonstration of

God's power among weak human vessels.

Paul and the other New Testament apostles exhorted us to begin the journey into the "deep things of God" here and now (1 Cor. 2:10). Such motivating knowledge equips believers to be all that they can be and to become able ambassadors of Christ in this world.

> However, we speak wisdom among those who are mature, yet not the wisdom of this age, nor of the rulers of this age, who are coming to nothing. But we speak the wisdom of God in a mystery, the hidden wisdom which God ordained before the ages for our glory, which none of the rulers of this age knew; for had they known, they would not have crucified the Lord of glory.
>
> But as it is written: "Eye has not seen, nor ear heard, nor have entered into the heart of man the things which God has prepared for those who love Him." But God has revealed them to us through His Spirit. For the Spirit searches all things, yes, the deep things of God. For what man knows the things of a man except the spirit of the man which is in him? Even so no one knows the things of God except the Spirit of God. Now we have received, not the spirit of the world, but the Spirit who is from God, that we might know the things that have been freely given to us by God.
>
> These things we also speak, not in words which man's wisdom teaches but which the Holy Spirit teaches, comparing spiritual things with spiritual. But the natural man does not receive the things of the Spirit of God, for they are foolishness to him; nor can he know them, because they are spiritually discerned.

> But he who is spiritual judges all things, yet he him-
> self is rightly judged by no one. For "who has known
> the mind of the Lord that he may instruct Him?" But
> we have the mind of Christ.
>
> —1 CORINTHIANS 2:6–16

After referring to his power evangelism strategy, the apostle begins to speak about the foreordained "hidden wisdom" of God, which directly relates to the divine beautification of our redeemed human lives—"for our glory" (v. 7). This "wisdom" is all to do with genuine *prophetic revelation*. The very "mystery" of God (v. 7) is progressively revealed to human beings who are "in Christ." God has designed the human spirit to thrive on being touched and upon touching the mystery of God.

Too often in the history of the church, Christians have been apologetic for the mysteries of our faith, rather than capitalizing upon them. Now, at least in the western cultures, *rationalism* and the *secular humanism* that was spawned by it have stripped from our societies a spiritual consciousness.

At times, the church in the West has been a primary agent of wrongly "demystifying" the gospel in the eyes of multitudes of our citizens. Some of this pressure came from a false dichotomy that arose between popular scientific theories of the mid-twentieth century and biblical theology. Ironically, the scientific community of today, by means of more powerful microscopes and telescopes and many archeological breakthroughs, is discovering facts that are undermining many of these past notions about the universe. The obviously intelligent, grand and vast design in the universe is making belief in God and His power quite a bit more popular among scientists these days. If the church hadn't bent herself backward to accommodate popular science in the past, then we would be standing on much better evangelistic ground today. As such, the body of Christ has to regain much lost credibility in order to be taken seriously by many serious-minded people.

The liberal wing of the church of the twentieth century called into question the veracity of the virgin birth, the miracles of Christ, the historicity of Jesus, heaven and hell, Christ's bodily resurrection and His future bodily return to earth. The fundamentalist wing of the church of the twentieth century, although remaining true to these essential doctrines, denuded the church of spiritual power through cessationism. Both wings tampered with and truncated the gospel of Jesus Christ.

One ironic result of this has been the reemergence of a spiritual hunger in our Western culture. Ultimately, the longing within the human soul to touch transcendent spiritual power cannot be effectively suppressed in the cycles of a society. However, many of these people have turned their hearts and eyes toward Eastern mysticism because the form of Christianity to which they were exposed denied the biblical belief in the miraculous power of God being accessible to us and very relevant to our earthly existence. What the church consciously and willingly sacrificed to create a more sterile and controllable environment for herself and her membership has backfired upon her!

Now we have the dubious task of apologizing to the unbelieving world for our own unbelief—"Well, actually God *isn't* dead after all." Or, "It seems that the Holy Spirit actually *is still* in the miracle business. Sorry about that!" We should have stuck to the Scriptures in the first place.

I had a somewhat humorous prophetic dream a few years ago that I find simply marvelous. I saw multitudes of people around the world streaming to faith in the Lord Jesus Christ and to join His church. These people had been caught up in the New Age Movement. But through various means, they had become exposed to the superior power and love of God being demonstrated through the church of Jesus Christ. The inferior powers and shallow interpersonal relationships of the counterfeit kingdom had left them quite empty. They were touched and blessed by the superior power, but it was ultimately the superior love they witnessed among Christians that had sold them on Christianity. There were millions of them. As I was suddenly awakened out of this dream, I heard a voice say, "Tell them that I am the Ghost with the most!"

I knew that this was to be our message to this generation. In the past, the Western church has basically said, "There's no such thing as ghosts." When I was a young boy, this was a common saying conveniently used by tired parents to calm their frightened kids. Unfortunately, it simply isn't true. There is a *spirit world,* and we should equip our children to deal with it when it manifests—for good or evil.

Our message to this generation needs to be, "Yes, there is some power in the New Age Movement, but it is a deceptive, inferior power. There is a greater and altogether good divine power available to us through faith in Jesus Christ. Only He can truly satisfy your spiritual thirst and connect you to the power of God."

Those things, which *in times past* were *hidden* from humanity, have *now* been *revealed* to believers in Christ by the Spirit of God. The Holy Spirit is the only Person who knows the depths of the heavenly Father's heart, but He is not hoarding this insight. He is the very Spirit whom we have freely received. In fact, He is sharing the heart of God richly with us, for this is His primary function in these New Covenant times:

> However, when He, the Spirit of truth, has come, He will guide you into all truth; for He will not speak on His own authority, but whatever He hears He will speak; and He will tell you things to come. He will glorify Me, for He will take of what is Mine and declare it to you. All things that the Father has are Mine. Therefore I said that He will take of Mine and declare it to you.
>
> —JOHN 16:13–15

The apostle goes on to say that this same Spirit of revelation empowers us to speak what He has revealed to us—He provides both inspired *thoughts* and inspired *utterances* so that we can communicate divine truth to others via His power working through us (1 Cor. 2:13). This, of course, is an excellent definition of how prophetic ministry operates.

Paul concludes the chapter by rhetorically inquiring, just as Isaiah did, if anyone has known the mind of the Lord in such a way that they could be His instructor (1 Cor. 2:16). Naturally, no one in the universe qualifies for such a role.

However, despite this limitation, Paul says that we do "have the mind of Christ." This is a brilliant way to describe the essence of prophetic ministry. In 1 Corinthians 2, Paul covers the bases of the preaching of the prophetic gospel—receiving prophetic revelation, speaking that revelation forth under the inspiration of the Holy Spirit and possessing the very mind of Christ. This is why I believe this chapter to be the greatest chapter in the Bible regarding prophetic ministry.

FIVE PRIMARY BLESSINGS OF THE PROPHETIC MINISTRY

1. The prophetic ministry is a source of spiritual
    life and purpose.

> But He answered and said, "It is written, 'Man shall
> not live by bread alone, but by every word that pro-
> ceeds from the mouth of God.'"
>
> —MATTHEW 4:4

God's word is food for the human soul. To live a full
human life, we must not eat only natural food for our
bodies, but we must also hear and do the word of God.
Of course, Holy Scripture has been given to us as the primary source of God's truth. Every other way in which it
comes to us is secondary and to be subordinated to its
supreme revelation. However, God can and does speak
to us in many ways—dreams, visions, voices, angels,
visitations, inspired utterances, inner knowings, sermons,
art and literature, natural events, spiritual phenomena
and the like. Prophetic experiences are an important
means of our hearing from God. Any way in which He
chooses to send His word to us is precious and becomes
vital nourishment for our lives. We live by *every word* that
proceeds from His mouth.

It is by the word of God "coming" to us that meaning,
dignity and access to the divine kingdom are imparted to
us. In the following passage, Jesus quotes Psalm 82:

> Jesus answered them, "Is it not written in your law,
> 'I said, "You are gods"'? If He called them gods, to
> whom the word of God came (and the Scripture
> cannot be broken), do you say of Him whom the

Father sanctified and sent into the world, 'You are blaspheming,' because I said, 'I am the Son of God'?"

—JOHN 10:34–36

Upon a close examination of both texts, several things become clear. First, Jesus is not saying that humans are divine. He is referring to the calling and capacity that God has granted people to share in His rule and dominion—a "god-like" function. Second, He is saying that this connection with divine purpose comes to mere humans by means of "the word of God" coming to them. It is the reception of God's word that lifts us up from our fallen dustiness and quickens us to interface with the powers of heaven itself. Third, even though the word of God comes to us, it is no guarantee that we will fulfill the potential for which it has been sent. The princes referred to in Psalm 82 failed to heed the word that they received from God and fell under His judgment. Therefore, receiving divine revelation should humble us rather than cause us to boast in ourselves. *Prophetic revelation is a divine invitation that requires a faithful human response in order for it to achieve its full intention.*

This principle is what the writer of Hebrews alludes to in the passage below:

Therefore, since a promise remains of entering His rest, let us fear lest any of you seem to have come short of it. For indeed the gospel was preached to us as well as to them; but the word which they heard did not profit them, not being mixed with faith in those who heard it.

—HEBREWS 4:1–2

2. Prophetic ministry is a source of conviction
    and the sense of the immediacy of God.

> But if all prophesy, and an unbeliever or an unin-
> formed person comes in, he is convinced by all, he is
> convicted by all. And thus the secrets of his heart are
> revealed; and so, falling down on his face, he will
> worship God and report that God is truly among you.
> —1 CORINTHIANS 14:24–25

Often the "secret of the Lord" is imbedded within a genuine prophetic word. When people are confronted with the
fact that God knows the details of their lives and thoughts,
many times a spiritual chemistry change transpires within
that person. I love to ponder the story of Jesus and
Nathaniel in John 1:45–51. Philip had gone to tell Nathaniel
that he had discovered the Christ, and Nathaniel expressed
his pain and cynicism by replying, "Can anything good
come out of Nazareth?" However, when Jesus saw him
coming near, He called out, "Behold, an Israelite indeed, in
whom is no deceit." When Nathaniel asked Jesus how He
knew him, Jesus simply answered, "Before Philip called
you, when you were under the fig tree, I saw you."

Nathaniel then answered, "Rabbi, You are the Son of
God! You are the King of Israel!"

At this point, it almost seems that Jesus is somewhat
amazed at Nathaniel's extravagant response of faith. Jesus
answered and said to him, "Because I said to you, 'I saw
you under the fig tree,' do you believe? You will see
greater things than these." And He said to him, "Most
assuredly, I say to you, hereafter you shall see heaven
open, and the angels of God ascending and descending
upon the Son of Man."

This account causes me to wonder what Nathaniel was doing or saying under that fig tree. Maybe he was praying something like, "God, are You really there? Do You see me under this fig tree? When are You going to send Messiah to our nation? Let me know somehow that You are listening to me." And although Nathaniel expresses his doubting words to Philip, when Jesus sees him, He sees beyond the doubts to Nathaniel's heart of integrity that went deeper than the doubts. A simple prophetic "word of knowledge" released Nathaniel's heart to believe and worship with great passion. Jesus promised that he would see even greater power than this in the days that would follow.

A few years ago, I was ministering in eastern Canada at a conference. I was dining with several couples who were in leadership in the body of Christ in that region. We were discussing the prophetic ministry, and at one point they asked me about any experiences I might have had with "prophetic evangelism." I told them that just a couple of months previously I had had the privilege of leading a lady named JoJo to the Lord during a public service at Immanuel Church in Romford, England. Early that morning I had received a spiritual dream about a piece of ripe fruit falling into my hand, and I intuitively knew that someone was going to come to faith that morning during the service. I asked one of the leaders of the church if there were any non-Christians present in the gathering that morning. He pointed JoJo and another person out to me during the singing part of our worship. As I watched JoJo, I saw the Holy Spirit moving upon her. I interrupted the singing and gently led JoJo to Jesus that morning right in front of the whole congregation. She wept for joy that day as Jesus washed away the guilt of her sins.

Just as I was relating this testimony to the people at my

table, I received a vision of our waiter, Eric. I saw the Lord reaching out to him with open arms, and I saw the love in Christ's eyes for this young man. I knew that God was drawing him near to Himself in this season of his life. Then I said to my friends, "The Lord is going to give us a token on the spot of His promise that we will see more prophetic evangelism in the coming days."

When Eric came to serve us again, I said to him, "I don't want to frighten you in any way, but I just received a vision from God's Holy Spirit about you."

Before I could say anything else, he blurted out, "My parents are missionaries."

I kindly replied, "That's wonderful. Are you walking with the Lord right now?" He said that he had fallen away from his faith in God, so I inquired, "Have you been thinking about coming back to Christ recently?"

"I've actually been thinking about it a lot," he said.

"How about coming back to Jesus right now?" I asked.

"OK," he replied simply.

I said, "Welcome back. The Lord loves you very much." I trust that Eric found his way back into Christian fellowship, for I have never seen or heard from him since.

The prophetic word of God has a marvelous ability to penetrate the wrong defenses of the human mind and soul. Many times prophetic utterances are attended with a sense of God's nearness. True prophecy is a kingdom event—the eternal presence and power of God break in on us here and now in time and space. Such words can serve to connect us to God's transcendent majesty.

3. Prophetic ministry is a source of courage and insight for our spiritual warfare.

> This charge I commit to you, son Timothy, according
> to the prophecies previously made concerning you,
> that by them you may wage the good warfare.
> —1 TIMOTHY 1:18

Here in this verse Paul categorically states that prophecies are an important weapon in our arsenal for the spiritual warfare in which we are engaged—"*by them* you may wage a good warfare." The New Testament presents a picture that a true Christian's whole earthly life is being played out on a cosmic stage—"for we have been made a spectacle to the world, both to angels and to men" (1 Cor. 4:9). God is telling a melodramatic story to angels, demons and all humanity through each of our lives.

Many believers have a too narrow view of spiritual warfare. The scope of the real battlefield is very broad, our resources are powerful and vast and the battle cannot be delayed or ignored. We will either engage the enemy or become prisoners of war—there is no neutral zone. Fortunately, it is a "*good* fight" (2 Tim. 4:7). Our spiritual adrenalin kicks in as we run to the battle. And delightfully surprising, we can be waging a mighty war while we are enjoying and living out the ordinary things of daily life for the glory of God: studying, singing, eating, playing, working, sleeping, loving our spouses and children, fellowshiping, praying, sharing our faith, laying our hands on the sick, feeding the poor, laughing, weeping, giving, listening, talking, teaching, encouraging others or simply "just being there" for someone.

Most of the time it doesn't even seem or feel like a war at all. But as we do whatever God has called us to do at any given moment through the strength that He provides, we are dealing powerful blows against the hosts of evil and taking territory for our glorious King. Our warfare is not carnal or physically violent—it is a war of love, truth, righteousness, joy and peace making.

> And whatever you do in word or deed, do all in the name of the Lord Jesus, giving thanks to God the Father through Him.
> —COLOSSIANS 3:17

> For though we walk in the flesh, we do not war according to the flesh. For the weapons of our warfare are not carnal but mighty in God for pulling down strongholds, casting down arguments and every high thing that exalts itself against the knowledge of God, bringing every thought into captivity to the obedience of Christ, and being ready to punish all disobedience when your obedience is fulfilled.
> —2 CORINTHIANS 10:3–6

We cannot live a healthy Christian life or function rightly in the church without adopting a "wartime" mentality. The sacrifices we are called to embrace will seem too great to make if we don't understand that we are involved in the most awesome war the universe has ever known. It is during wartimes that people understand sacrificial lifestyles simply as necessary, reasonable and wise.

Prophetic revelation can equip us to wage a more effective war. It serves as "secret intelligence" for the battle strategies. It provides "smart bombs" that specifically target the strongholds of evil within or without. It brings with it *discernment* into the purposes of God, our own motives, the hearts of people and the schemes of Satan. When Jesus faced the devil's temptations in the wilderness, the spirit of prophecy came upon Him to "tailor" the Word of God to the situation.

The evil one quoted, but twisted and misapplied, the Holy Scriptures in his attempt to draw Jesus into disobedience to His Father. However, Jesus was given just the right Scriptures, which He had surely hidden in His heart from the time of His youth, to effectively counter and fight off the deceit of the devil. Paul Cain has said that the Scriptures are the "favorite chariot" within which the Holy Spirit likes to "ride" as He delivers to us the "word of the Lord." The memorizing of and meditation upon the Scriptures provides the Spirit "material to work with" in order to help us under pressure. After all, the Word of God is the Spirit's sword.

The warfare we face is significantly invisible, although it regularly manifests in the natural realm. However, we become so accustomed to what we see with our eyes that we often don't recognize the subtle presence of the demonic at work. We really need the "deeper sight" that prophetic discernment brings to us in order to get to the root of many problems in our lives and in this world. Although Satan does work *directly* at times, he normally enjoys working *indirectly* through the more familiar things, structures and events all around us that serve as camouflage for his dark works. The typical arenas of his activity are "the world" and "the flesh."

From their cosmic strongholds in heavenly places, Satan and his ranks of dark princes work by every means possible, from perpetrating outright evil all the way up to twisting good things, to establishing "strongholds" within individuals, families, congregations of believers and the ungodly cultures around them. In this way, Satan carries on his spiteful war against the powers of heaven and the saints of God.

If Christians will deal courageously with personal, familial and congregational strongholds and then boldly take a stand in truth, love and good works against cultural strongholds, then God will send true revival—overthrowing cosmic strongholds through the primary agency of His angelic powers. We cannot expect to effectively change the world or the cosmos unless we cooperate with God in making the changes that are more directly under our personal authority—"casting down arguments and every high thing that exalts itself against the knowledge of God, bringing every thought into captivity to the obedience of Christ, and *being ready to punish all disobedience when your obedience is fulfilled*" (2 Cor. 10:5–6, emphasis added). Obedience to God from the heart is the key to effective warfare, and prophetic revelation aids us in knowing God's will and heart more specifically.

A subtle satanic stronghold was gradually established in my soul as a young minister. In carnal reaction to the pain of some disappointments in my early years of pastoral ministry, I began relying more and more on my learned abilities and natural talents in conducting my ministry. I began to "play it safe" rather than allowing the anointing of the Holy Spirit to work through me as I had allowed at the beginning of my ministry. Many strongholds of evil are erected in our lives by such fleshly reactions to the pains and disappointments of living life in a fallen world and an imperfect church. About ten years ago, the Lord began to deal with the *self-reliance* that was significantly in control of my service for Him.

One night I had a vivid spiritual dream in which Jesus appeared to me. He was sitting on a great throne. He summoned me to come and kneel before Him. To my astonishment and chagrin, as I did, a stack of transparencies came forth from my belly and landed in my hands. I instantly knew that they were "my plans." I also knew that He saw right through them as I now could and that they were woefully inadequate. I then watched His face as He clearly said to me, "You have been waiting to obey Me until you had comprehensive plans. I want you to obey Me without comprehensive plans."

Through the years, I had come to believe that God expects us to have all of our ministry vision, plans and strategies clearly laid out in order to hit the right mark. Although I am in favor of people getting a vision for their lives and ministries, in my case I had taken it to an extreme and used my lack of clarity regarding the future as an excuse for not boldly and aggressively serving my Lord. I had allowed uncertainties to paralyze me with carnal fear.

In the dream, I bowed my head and wept. I said, "Lord, I don't want to be disobedient to You." After a minute or so, I looked up at Him through my tears and saw Him smiling at me. With this, the dream ended. This experience left an indelible imprint upon my soul, and with God's help, I have been more boldly obeying Him despite the continual presence of many uncertainties. As I have done so, the Lord has continued to increase the release of His spiritual authority through my life. This is the essence of "walking by faith and not by sight." Some people gravitate to the prophetic because they secretly imagine that it will negate this principle. They couldn't be farther from the truth! By this prophetic dream and the precise discernment it has provided for me, I have been much better equipped to tear down the stronghold of self-reliance in which I used to find a false refuge.

4. Prophetic ministry is a source of the knowledge of divine timing and guidance.

> As they ministered to the Lord and fasted, the Holy Spirit said, "Now separate to Me Barnabas and Saul for the work to which I have called them." Then, having fasted and prayed, and laid hands on them, they sent them away. So, being sent out by the Holy Spirit, they went down to Seleucia, and from there they sailed to Cyprus.
>
> —ACTS 13:2–4

Out of this time of intensely ministering to the Lord and seeking His face with prayer and fasting, the Holy Spirit broke in upon these prophets and teachers and commissioned two men from among their number to go forth as apostles—"sent ones." This was the right time, and these were the right men. As a result, the course of human history was significantly changed for centuries to come as Paul and Barnabas set out on their first missionary journey.

It was through some kind of unstated prophetic experience that the Lord Jesus Christ initiated this mission. These apostles were launched behind the enemy's lines like guided missiles through the release of a strategic prophetic communication. It is possible that Barnabas and Paul already knew that God had called them to this mission, and the prophetic experience was a confirmation to them. Nevertheless, they were waiting on the Lord's proper timing for their commissioning. Sometimes *the calling* and *the commission* are years apart in the lives of God's servants.

It is interesting to note that even if this word was not a confirmation to a previously known divine calling, it came in the context of earnest seeking and team ministry.

Even after the believers at Antioch received the revelation, they prayed and fasted before laying their hands upon Barnabas and Saul to send them out. Great care must be taken in the stewarding of such heavy prophecy. To be guided by prophetic experience is a very delicate spiritual art. I will address this more in the next chapter.

One important lesson that we can learn from this narrative in Acts 13 is that we really do need to hear more specifically from God about the nature and timing of our service for Him. From one angle, someone might say, "Well, didn't Jesus tell us all to 'go and preach the good news to every creature'? Why not just go anywhere or everywhere at anytime and do it? Why does it matter exactly where we go or when we go?" The prophets and teachers here in Antioch knew about the general commission that Jesus gave to the whole church. Still, they approached this mission very soberly and deliberately.

The point is that we need the ministry of the Holy Spirit to "tailor" the generally revealed will of God specifically to our lives, circumstances and ministries. Of course, obeying the generally revealed will of God is the best thing that we can do to position ourselves to receive more specific guidance from the Holy Spirit. At critical junctures in our lives, we can pray and expect God to make His will more specific to us. If this kind of prophetic insight doesn't come, then we must plow ahead and make the wisest choices possible. However, God will often provide such insight if we learn to look for and expect the subjective signals—a dream or a vision, an unshakeable impression, a message through a natural event, an answered prayer, an open door or even a closed door. The Lord will teach us the art of interpreting these kinds of things as we walk closely to Him through the years.

One time when Paul Cain visited a particular gathering of Christians, he asked the Lord, "Father, what are You doing here in this place?"

Immediately the Spirit of God responded to his question, "Nothing. And don't you try anything either."

Paul has been a wonderful example to many who are being raised up into prophetic ministry in this generation. He has learned the discipline of holding prophetic information until such a time as the Holy Spirit might release him to prophesy with authority.

There is a well-known saying in our culture—"Timing is everything." During a particular interaction with the Lord, I felt that He was adapting this saying to me through the Spirit: "Timing isn't everything, but it almost is." In one of my talks with Paul, he described one of the ways in which the Lord has dealt with him on timing in prophetic ministry. On many occasions the Spirit of God has said to him in relation to a specific issue about which he would be asking the Lord, "Keep your ear close to the door and wait." Sometime later regarding that issue the Spirit would say, "Not yet." Then at a later point he would hear, "Now." At certain times, when for various reasons that opportunity was not capitalized upon, he would hear the Holy Spirit say, "Too late." Sometimes, by the mercy of God, this cycle would repeat itself regarding the very same situation.

5. Prophetic ministry is a source of supernatural healing power.

And in Lystra a certain man without strength in his feet was sitting, a cripple from his mother's womb, who had never walked. This man heard Paul speaking. Paul, observing him intently and seeing that he had faith to be healed, said with a loud voice, "Stand up straight on your feet!" And he leaped and walked.

—ACTS 14:8–10

Both in the Gospels and the Book of Acts, we regularly see prophetic revelation working in tandem with healing power. This dynamic is seen in the above passage. Paul received a prophetic discernment regarding the kind of faith that was operating in this crippled man. Obviously, the Holy Spirit was anointing Paul in this moment, and he simply and prophetically proclaimed this man's miraculous healing. This is prophetic intercession at its best!

THE STEADMANS' STORY

My colleagues, Don and Julie Steadman, with whom I have served in ministry for over ten years, had a remarkable and life-altering experience with the power of the Holy Spirit. What follows is Don's account of how prophetic ministry sparked both his own infilling of the Spirit and the miraculous healing of their daughter.

> My wife, Julie, and I visited Metro Christian Fellowship (South Kansas City Fellowship at the time) a few times right after it first started in 1982, but quickly left it because its "spiritual culture" just seemed too strange for our liking. The "prophetic ministry" in particular at this fellowship was hard for us to understand. We decided to return to our conservative evangelical church.
>
> In December of 1993, during the eighth month of Julie's pregnancy with our second child, our doctor became concerned that the baby wasn't growing

93

properly and ordered some tests to be run. The tests showed that our baby had a severely enlarged kidney. I remember the medical evaluation of the kidney stated that it was "two to three times the standard deviation." The doctor told us that the best we could hope for was that our baby would have Down's syndrome, a chromosome problem that can be fatal to the child.

Six months earlier, a couple in our Bible study, who had the same doctor as ours, had a child who was born with the same condition. The baby was born with all sorts of complications and passed away in the first week of its life.

As we faced our crisis, we thought about calling Mike Bickle. We needed a miracle, and we knew that the church he pastored believed in prayer. Julie and I wrestled with God in prayer about making this call, and we finally came to a place of peace, even though we still had no theological grid for supernatural healing. We simply felt that the Lord would, through their prayers, give us the grace either to live with the fact of having a handicapped child or courageously face the death of our child. We called Mike and arranged for some friends who belonged to the church already to meet with us and Mike so we could pray together in his office before the Tuesday night service. We arrived there about 6:30 P.M. (the meeting was at 7), and our time for prayer was very limited.

When we entered the room, Mike introduced two men who were there, telling us they were prophetic and that we were going to see if the Lord had anything to say to us through their ministry. They sat us in two chairs in the middle of the room, laid hands on us and began to prophesy.

Nothing about the atmosphere felt weird at all. As they shared their impressions, Mike would stop them to ask questions. It was a very comfortable, loving environment. One of the men, a short Hispanic man, laid hands on my head. As he did, the power of God went right through my head. The first thing he said was that God had allowed this circumstance to happen for our good. The men's prophetic words to me were very direct—they were the secrets of my heart. Even though it was direct, and at times almost rebuking (though in a kind way), it was liberating for me. It set me free.

Then they prophesied over Julie for a little while with the same results. Finally, having to rush out of the room to start the service, they laid hands on the baby and prayed for it. Within fifteen to twenty seconds after they began praying, they said that there was nothing wrong with the child, that the child was absolutely perfect. When they said that, something happened within me, and I don't know how to explain it except to say that faith was released in me. I knew that what they said was true. I was totally sure.

They left the room, and I began speaking uncontrollably in tongues, though no one had said anything about tongues. As a high school kid years earlier, someone had told me I needed to speak in tongues. So I'd tried. I still don't know how real that was. But this experience was undeniable—the language just flowed out of me and wouldn't stop, even to the point that I was somewhat embarrassed about it.

It was six more weeks before Amy was born. The medical tests continued to show that there were problems, but when she was born on January 9, 1984, *she came out in perfect health.* There were specialists from the children's hospital in the delivery room, lots of people. When she was born, the doctor looked at her and said, "My, she looks fine. Looks like your prayers were answered."

A specialist examined her and said virtually the same thing—"She's perfect."

Two days later, our pediatrician said, "I have to run tests. The documented prenatal medical reports (of which we have copies) are so conclusive that I have to find out if everything's OK." He ran the tests, and sure enough, everything checked out perfectly. We had a healthy baby born, and we were introduced to the prophetic ministry, which in our case God used as a powerful catalyst for a miracle. We have no doubt to this day that a genuine miracle of healing took place in Amy. These events significantly transformed our lives from that day until today. Since then, I have witnessed hundreds of accurate and helpful prophetic words given through Spirit-filled men, women and even children to build up the body of Christ.

Spiritual vitality, conviction and a sense of God's nearness, courage and insight for spiritual warfare, divine guidance and healing power—although this is clearly not an exhaustive list, these are five marvelous blessings that flow to redeemed humanity through wisely stewarded prophetic experiences. Again, we need to remember how precious this prophetic anointing and ministry of the Spirit is in order to face the perils that also attend its operation among imperfect human vessels.

Chapter 4

PERILS OF THE PROPHETIC

A GOOD BEGINNING POINT when seeking to identify necessary safeguards around something powerful is to contemplate "worst-case scenarios" and then work back from that point to help identify and insure the proper use of that powerful thing—something like the prophetic ministry. In this chapter, I want to discuss some of the dangers that have in the past—and may continue to do so—attended the belief and practice of prophetic ministry in the church.

DIVISIONS IN THE CHURCH

If every believer can potentially hear directly from God and speak on His behalf, then what happens when two believers disagree about what God is saying? Multiply this dynamic by more than two, and things can get spiritually and relationally complicated very quickly. The typical task of spiritual leaders is to discern truth, half-truths and error. But they must also seek to reconcile personal relationships that have fallen on hard times. On one hand, they run the risk of offending one or more of their followers. On the other hand, they must guard against offending the Holy Spirit Himself.

People are often highly emotional about the words for which they claim direct divine inspiration. They feel as if their personal integrity is on the line, and they are very defensive about being generally right, if not totally accurate. It's embarrassing enough to be wrong about something. It's exponentially embarrassing to be wrong "in the name of God." To correct them in this arena, even gently so, can be very difficult.

Some sincere people have the conception that they are hearing almost constantly directly from God. Many have been taught that God is always "talking," but that most Christians just aren't good listeners. They really believe that if they become sensitive and mature enough they will be in a constant direct dialogue with God. In light of this, many purpose in their hearts to be different than those so dull of hearing. Their sincerity can be counterproductive. They try too hard to "read God's mind," and they begin to fantasize that they are hearing from God although He is not actually speaking to them. It's virtually impossible to lead a group of people into long-term healthy relationships and unity within the church who deeply believe that they're often and infallibly hearing the voice of God. I overheard a wise prophetic servant of God say, "God isn't talking half as much as some people think He is, and when He does speak, He means it twice as much as most people think He does!"

HERO WORSHIP

One of the historic problems accompanying various out-pourings of God's power has been the tendency for people to exalt in wrong ways the human vessels God uses. Some of these catalytic members of the body have tried to keep this from happening, while others have enjoyed it and capitalized upon it. I believe that this has actually quenched some divine visitations and caused the Lord to lift His grace and power off of those movements. Rank-and-file members of the body of Christ are often paralyzed from doing the Lord's ministry because they are waiting for the "anointed ones" to do it. They feel that these special people are the only ones qualified to function in the Lord's power. If we insist on putting people on pedestals, then we are only helping to set them up for a fall. It's not all wrong to have "heroes," but we have to understand the dangers that accompany hero worship and counter the downside of the dynamics it can create.

God raises up people to "champion" various divine causes, but the rest of us are supposed to be inspired to rise up to partner with them in ministry—not stand in awe of them and watch them do it all. That isn't healthy for them or for us, and it short-circuits God's intentions. This seems to be especially true with the more obviously supernatural and spectacular gifts of healing, miracles and prophetic revelation.

We must learn from history and allow the Lord to help us find a new paradigm of interpreting and utilizing these kinds of anointed human vessels. The supernatural ministry must become more and more a normal part of healthy church life and be more widely distributed among the rank-and-file members of the body of Christ. Specially anointed leaders should find ways to recognize and nurture these giftings within others. They must learn to take the Lord and His work seriously without taking themselves too seriously. If a generation of gifted leaders will arise who refuse to climb on the pedestals that others are so often willing to build for them, then maybe the Lord will grant a visitation that will come and stay—rather than come and go.

OVERRELIANCE ON PROPHECY FOR PERSONAL GUIDANCE

The reality of the prophetic power of God can be very emotionally intoxicating to us. Once people experience it and are benefited, sometimes greatly, from it, they are tempted to think that it is supposed to operate for them in every situation of life. This is a big mistake. God is a father, not a dictator. Sometimes He will dictate orders to us in the broader context of fathering us. But more profoundly, He wants to transform us within so that we "catch" His thoughts and feelings by becoming more like Him and having His attitudes and perspectives incorporated deeply into the fiber of our beings. He wants us to "prove" His good, acceptable and perfect will through the "renewing of our minds" more than by guiding us by the gift of prophecy (Rom. 12:1–2).

Most often, prophecy functions to confirm what the Lord is already subtly impressing upon our (or others') hearts and minds. We can learn this application from the account of Elijah's running for his life in reaction to Jezebel's death threat against him.

> And behold, the LORD passed by, and a great and
> strong wind tore into the mountains and broke the

100

> rocks in pieces before the LORD, but the LORD was
> not in the wind; and after the wind an earthquake,
> but the LORD was not in the earthquake; and after
> the earthquake a fire, but the LORD was not in the
> fire; and after the fire *a still small voice.*
> —I KINGS 19:11–12, EMPHASIS ADDED

Elijah was a man who knew the dramatic power of God. A few days before this time, during an awesome spiritual showdown on Mount Carmel, God was in the fire! Yet, immediately after this great spiritual victory during which Elijah had prophetically called down fire from heaven to prove the superior power of *YHWH* over Baal, he ran away in fear and self-protection rather than completing the work God had apparently assigned to him—overseeing the execution of Jezebel herself and leading Israel into a great revival. After Elijah had run a long way, the Lord confronted him with his failure. At this point in Elijah's personal journey, the Lord wasn't in the earthquake, the whirlwind or the fire. Rather, he came in a "still, small voice." Powerful encounters and experiences do not ensure the obedience of those to whom they come. At their best, they are simply divine invitations to obedience. It was by the less dramatic means of divine whispering that God communicated His will to Elijah.

People who have experienced or witnessed the dramatic guidance of the Holy Spirit in operation sometimes conclude that this is or should be considered the *normative way* for the Spirit to lead us through life's decisions. I have had many experiences with people who have imagined that they are hearing God's voice almost continually. I remember one young man who thought that God was telling him what to wear each day, what to eat, exactly where to go and when to go there, exactly what to say and so forth. However, he was unwilling to work or go to school. He was "mooching" off of his friends and fellow Christians. He was presenting himself as a minister of God, but the confusion around his thoughts, words and deeds was evident to everyone around him. He was not being a good witness to unbelievers or believers. Somehow he had gotten the idea that this method of guidance was what truly spiritual people experienced. He was actually obsessed and demonically oppressed. Still, he would not receive correction, even from the people who he agreed had walked longer and deeper with the Lord than he had.

The New Testament never instructs us to expect to receive our primary and/or daily guidance from such supernatural "fireworks"—although God is certainly able and willing to provide them from time to time. We are not called to be *automatons* of God that are clearly instructed in a mechanical way concerning every detail of the owner's desired behavior for the robot.

God wants to integrate His heart, mind and will into our souls and through our bodies in a *psychologically sound* way. That is, He wants us to intelligently want, internally desire and personally own His will for us. The communication of this will of God is often a gradual and more thorough process than just receiving verbal orders. God wants to *form* us in the process of *informing* us, and in fact, this personal formation takes precedence over the acquisition of knowledge.

I think of divine guidance as a *"dance* with our *guide."* It is not "goose-stepping" to an angry, impatient and verbose drill instructor. Like the prophetic ministry, guidance is more of an *art* than an *exact science.* It's more about a deeper relational intimacy with God than it is about specific details and knowledge. This concept of guidance is very important for prophetically oriented people to embrace. Otherwise, they will ultimately become disillusioned and can even inadvertently teach others to hold wrong expectations about how God's guidance will normally come to them.

For some, the prophetic gift appears to be a shortcut to guidance in contrast to the longer route of praying, searching the Scriptures, receiving wise counsel, suffering, character building, learning from experience and so forth. The truth is, as most people experienced in the prophetic can testify, this gift rarely works to guide the gifted persons themselves. Usually prophecy is given by the Spirit to minister confirmation to others. This is often very consternating to prophetically gifted people. God just isn't in as much of a hurry or panic to guide us as we usually are to get guided! He is "into" the journey as much as He is the destination. He is both a glorious intruder and a patient farmer. Seek to be guided by the more tried and true methods pioneered by the saints throughout the ages, and rejoice when the Spirit serendipitously intervenes with a clear word of prophecy to encourage you along the way.

Sometimes the Lord does graciously intervene with a prophetic word that gives us clear direction. He seems to do this more for some than for others. But be aware that as you start down the pathway, you will wish He would say more than He has! God gave Joseph some dreams that he then, in his immaturity, enthusiastically shared with the very people for whom their message wasn't very exciting at all. Sometimes God tells us just enough to get us into trouble!

103

> He sent a man before them—Joseph—who was sold
> as a slave. They hurt his feet with fetters, he was laid
> in irons. Until the time that his word came to pass,
> *the word of the Lord tested him.*
> —PSALM 105:17–19, EMPHASIS ADDED

The prophetic word of divine promise that comes to us will always be tested and refined in the fires of our experience. This kind of suffering will prepare us to walk into the promise with humility and gratitude working within our souls.

I would also add this word of caution. If someone gives you a prophecy that includes elements of guidance, do not allow it alone to move you. This kind of word needs to be confirmed by other sources, internal and/or external, before you should act upon it. God knows that we cannot allow the pressure that a lone prophecy may create to lead us. Pray about it, ask some wise friends to help you discern it, and if you have doubts about it, then "put it on the shelf" and wait for God to do something else that leads you to take it more seriously at a future date. If, after making these responses and a reasonable period of time goes by, this kind of word unduly distracts you from doing the things that you believe God has placed before you, toss it away—it was probably spurious in nature. I deeply believe that this kind of process is not a compromise, but a way of wisdom that honors the Lord and His word.

PERSONAL IDENTITY EASILY BECOMES WRAPPED AROUND GIFTING

Like with other giftings and ministries, it is very easy for prophetically gifted people to allow their basic identity to become wrongly entwined with their gifting. Other people will often reinforce this by "pulling" on them to give them "words." This relational, spiritual dynamic will initially energize those so gifted, but it doesn't last for long. Often, they will develop subtle ways to distance themselves from other people because of the pressure they feel. This is one way that self-protective and eccentric personality traits, methodologies in ministry and relational styles develop in them. This is often the reason that many prophetically gifted people have become somewhat bizarre and strange. In fact, they often consciously adopt such things as a way of enhancing their "prophetic persona." We must always seek to distinguish our gifts from our basic identity. We are foremost, and most profoundly, the servants and children of God. We are not our gifts. We receive and use gifts in our service to God and man, but they are not essential to who we are in relationship to our Creator and our brothers and sisters. Any other mentality is a recipe for great insecurity and weirdness.

Too Much of a Good Thing

> Do not be overly righteous, nor be overly wise: why should you destroy yourself?
> —Ecclesiastes 7:16

Indeed there can be "too much of a good thing." The prophetic can be abused, unused or overused. Because of the high impact and somewhat intoxicating nature of having the "voice of God" break into our experience, our excitement can lead us to imagine that God must want to release a prophetic word through us or someone else at almost any time we please. A form of hyperspirituality easily takes root in this kind of environment. On many occasions, people have literally demanded Paul Cain to "give them a word." The Spirit has given him a good comeback to this: "I'm sorry, I don't give 'command performances.'" Such a demand is the result of a "prophecy on demand" mentality. This almost smacks of the "psychic hotline" kind of thing that is becoming so popular in our time. The true prophetic ministry of Jesus Christ is far different from this shallow occultic counterfeit.

The quality of prophetic ministry that the Lord Jesus is jealous for is the kind that operates under the conscious anointing and presence of the Holy Spirit. It is possible for prophetic people to discern facts or to know something without having the permission or leading from the Spirit to give "a word" based around that information. When they do succumb to such pressure, the authority of the Lord will not be upon that word, and it may "fall to the ground" except for the mercy of God. The true prophetic is not essentially about *information*, but *impartation*.

It is hard for some people to grasp the fact that God can give a prophetic person information that either flows out of the gift itself or simply out of an intimacy with the Spirit that, nonetheless, is not to be communicated. Sometimes He just wants someone with whom He can share His burden. Sometimes He is calling them to intercede. Sometimes He is preparing them to deliver the word in its proper timing. Sometimes He is just training them in the basics of being sensitive to His voice.

Prophetic people who submit to the demands of people to give a word when the Spirit is not releasing the anointing will end up drying up and burning out. At some critical point, the oil in the lamp will be used up, and then the wick will start burning. That is, they will begin to prophesy out of their fleshly humanity, and the smoke and smell will ultimately not go unnoticed.

During any given time when genuine prophetic ministry is going forth, as a general rule it is safe to assume that God simply doesn't have "a word" for everyone in the gathering. Prophecy loses its chosen purpose when it becomes too common a thing. I am not intending to take potshots at any ministry that moves in a prophetic anointing, and I realize that this concept flies in the face of some common assumptions and practices in some of the Pentecostal/Charismatic movements. Yet, I believe that a warning like this needs to be sounded, and I would lovingly urge us all to seek the Lord more deeply on this matter. The "good" of the past can too easily become the enemy of the "best" that is being reserved for the days ahead.

OVEREXPOSURE

> But while he thought about these things, behold, an angel of the Lord appeared to him in a dream, saying, "Joseph, son of David, do not be afraid to take to you Mary your wife, for that which is conceived in her is of the Holy Spirit. And she will bring forth a Son, and you shall call His name JESUS, for He will save His people from their sins."
> —MATTHEW 1:20–21

Have you ever considered that when God visited the planet He chose to enter as a human embryo? Additionally, this happened only after many centuries of prophetically preparing the world for His arrival. Why didn't He just manifest Himself to humanity with a full manifestation of His excellent glory? The reason is because God knows the value of *subtlety*. Unfortunately, some people never do. God conceals His full glory for the sake of love. Humans would be totally undone and overwhelmed without any chance to "warm up" to encountering such power if God did not shield us from it to some degree.

In fact, the day is coming when the opportunity for such "warming up" will be over, and Jesus Christ will appear on the clouds of heaven in flaming fire as a fierce warrior who has come to judge the world in righteousness. That fire of God's glory will destroy all who have not embraced it at its "lower temperatures," provided by first "touching it" by faith (in contrast to sight) and by receiving the down payment of having fellowship with the fiery Holy Spirit who is sent to us from heaven.

The point is that God has progressively exposed His glory without overexposing it. Likewise, we must be careful not to assume that it is God's will for us constantly to "manifest" the Spirit who has been granted to dwell in each of us. He can peacefully live within us without perpetually flashing His power. Even the angels all around us don't "manifest" too often. Still sometimes, when they do, they disguise themselves and appear to be human.

We are not to become "prophecy machines" that have no *life* beyond the *gifting*. It is very difficult to relate in a healthy and loving way with people who are constantly striving to read God's mind and subjectively "tune in" to what the Spirit is saying. Frankly, this approach can get weird really fast. Certainly, there are times to press in to seek the Lord and wait upon Him with listening hearts. However, my experience has been that simply being with Him and adoring Him and then seeking to obey Him in the full range of my earthly life and responsibilities has positioned me to hear His voice at the appointed times.

When I have tried to get Him to "say something" to me, I have usually been frustrated.

God has normally prepared His prophetic vessels in the solitude of some kind of wilderness environment. Today, many people get their first taste of a season of prophetic anointing and immediately want to minister on platforms with microphone in hand! This kind of overexposure can be dangerous to all. God may choose to hide the glory inside of you for lengths of time and in various ways that may be confusing if you don't understand this principle. If He is presently choosing to hide you, find contentment in knowing Him, and let your roots go down deep into the rich soil of His transcendent kingdom. Then you will be ready to "manifest" in His perfect time. (See Isaiah 49.)

NEGLECT OF OTHER VITAL THINGS

The power of the prophetic can be exhilarating and thrilling—and so it should be. Hearing and speaking the true word of God is awesome by nature. It is, however, not a substitute for other aspects of Christian life and experience that are also ordained by God for our good and our growth. Sometimes people become so captivated by the prophetic that they become disinterested in these other vital things. The Scripture says that it is good to reach out to lay hold of one thing and yet not let go of the other.

> It is good that you grasp one thing, and also not let go of the other; for the one who fears God comes forth with both of them.
> —ECCLESIASTES 7:18, NAS

It is imperative that we embrace the reality of the

109

prophetic without neglecting the sometimes less intoxicating elements of our faith—praying, loving our spouse,
feeding the poor, studying, tithing, going to work, caring
for our children, paying our taxes, building healthy relationships and so forth. I have found that it is good for
prophetically gifted people to fully embrace and engage
in these other parts of life. It helps keep them in a greater
personal equilibrium.

PRIDE OF SUCCESS

There is probably no uglier form of pride than the kind that
so often becomes associated with giftedness. The classic
danger of a person or a people blessed by God is the constant danger of thinking and acting as if they've done
something to deserve it. The apostle Paul said, "What do
you have that you did not receive? Now if you did indeed
receive it, why do you boast as if you had not received it?"
(1 Cor. 4:7). We have what we have by the mercy of God.
This is especially true of spiritual giftings. This is, after all,
why God has called them "gifts!" So those who are helped
by the Holy Spirit clearly to hear and speak a true prophetic
word must be careful not to become arrogant about any
effectiveness they might come to enjoy.

EMBARRASSMENT OF FAILURE

Another but opposite problem that often surrounds the
prophetic is when people begin to "move out in faith"
and minister "words" to others. I can't imagine that any
Spirit-filled believer who has learned to minister prophetically effectively can claim that he or she has never
"missed it" at one time or another to some degree. Failure

is a normal part of any growth curve, and there are valuable lessons to learn by it. Of course, the embarrassment factor increases in the arena of failure in prophecy because of the intrinsic claim of divine inspiration that surrounds it. It is important to "back up" and get some healthy perspective on this issue so that the fear of failures—or the experience of them—does not paralyze us.

First, is prophecy valid or not? If we believe it is, then we must ask who is going to do it and how shall they begin. Shall we adopt such a rigorous philosophical and methodological standard that no mistakes will be tolerated—that is, anyone who errs in this area must automatically be shamed and labeled as false for "integrity's sake"? If we adopt this kind of mentality, it will only ensure that very few, if any, will venture into this ministry. (And that no one will do it long term!) I believe we must develop a practical prophetic "on-ramp" for learners that will not violate Scripture or true integrity, but that will also encourage people to take the proper and necessary risks that go with ministering prophecy.

"Use Me"—"I Feel Used" Contradiction

I have observed an ironic dynamic that can happen around prophetic people that would be humorous if it weren't so tragic. Some people have prayed for years that God would use them to move in prophecy. Then suddenly, almost mysteriously, He actually does it. They may begin to receive and remember dreams that contain revelatory content. Or they may see mental pictures with special meaning for the people for whom they pray. They experience thoughts invading their own thoughts, and as they share these thoughts with others, they discover that

God has spoken to them and through them.

At first this is an exhilarating experience that is spiritually and relationally motivating. After some time, they become known as prophetic people within their church communities. Soon a growing demand is placed inadvertently upon them to perform prophetically for their friends and for their friends' friends. Most of it happens, not on public platforms before hundreds, but in the presence of a few—often at very inconvenient times.

After a few years of this dynamic, these people begin to complain to God, "I feel used!" I can almost hear the Lord respond, "Isn't that what you prayed for?"

Obviously, there are loving and appropriate ways to manage this difficult dynamic to ensure that ministry doesn't grossly interfere with the other necessities and duties of life. However, it will never be managed to suit our fleshly "demand" for "perfectly ordered lives." Our lives will be interrupted many times if the Lord is gracious to manifest His life through ours by the power of the Holy Spirit.

CONTROL AND MANIPULATION

> Therefore, since through God's mercy we have this ministry, we do not lose heart. Rather, we have renounced secret and shameful ways; we do not use deception, nor do we distort the word of God. On the contrary, by setting forth the truth plainly we commend ourselves to every man's conscience in the sight of God.
>
> —2 CORINTHIANS 4:1–2, NIV

In this passage Paul sets forth the proper standards for motivation and methodology in ministry. First, he makes it clear that being continually aware that he is a recipient of the mercy of God is the secret to his perseverance and influence upon others through the ministry. For Paul, the issue at hand was more the Lord's ministry than his own. He was confident that the Lord was responsible to make His own influence felt by people. Paul's job was to be faithful to represent the Lord Jesus and His word humbly and honestly—no more and no less. Paul remembered why he was doing what he was doing, and this protected him from "cheating." He consciously and deliberately renounced utilizing unethical means of influencing others. He refused to stoop to manipulating and wrongly controlling others in the name of ministry. "Commending ourselves to other's consciences" has to do with trusting the Holy Spirit to communicate through our lives and words deep into the hearts and minds of people. If He will convince them of the truth that we live and speak, then they will be enabled safely to give their hearts to the Lord and to us, His ministers.

Unfortunately, many so-called ministers have compromised in this arena and thereby extorted affection, honor, money and commitments from people by means of their own persuasive abilities. This is the antithesis of genuine Christian ministry and leadership. Speaking on God's behalf is serious and powerful stuff, and we must steward this responsibility in the fear of God. This is especially true of prophetic ministry, which carries the claim of direct divine inspiration and revelation with it. If the gift of prophecy is abused and misused to manipulate others, then a day of reckoning will surely come, and "it won't be pretty!"

TRYING TO IMPRESS OTHERS

We all have enough personal insecurity within us to be

tempted with trying to impress other people. Hearing directly from God can be pretty downright impressive! When believers become recognized as being blessed with prophetic gifting, it is often challenging for them to stay humble before God and man. They must remind themselves that it is a gift that is in operation—not a sign of their spiritual maturity or intrinsic holiness. A right response to being used by God to minister His power should be toward a greater awareness of His majesty and our utter dependency upon Him. We should absolutely refuse to play the ego-centered social games that people often play to exalt themselves and put others down. Too often jealousy and competition fuel interpersonal relationships within the body of Christ. In many instances this is true of the way prophetically gifted members of the church relate to one another. But this is not the way of Christ. This is not the way of wisdom. We should delight in lowliness, servanthood and meekness. May the words of James, the Lord's brother, be branded upon our hearts:

> Who is wise and understanding among you? Let him show it by his good life, by deeds done in the humility that comes from wisdom. But if you harbor bitter envy and selfish ambition in your hearts, do not boast about it or deny the truth. Such "wisdom" does not come down from heaven but is earthly, unspiritual, of the devil. For where you have envy and selfish ambition, there you find disorder and every evil practice. But the wisdom that comes from heaven is first of all pure; then peace-loving, considerate, submissive, full of mercy and good fruit, impartial and sincere.
>
> —JAMES 3:13–17, NIV

TAKING OURSELVES TOO SERIOUSLY

There has to be a way that people can take God and His word seriously without taking themselves so seriously. Too often prophetic people come across to others as "ultra-intense" because of their relational style. Even though they may not philosophically believe that they're infallible, they act and speak as though they ought to be. I believe that it is important to teach prophetically gifted people to learn to lighten up a little. They aren't called to carry all the burdens of the world upon their shoulders. God has actually distributed that burden quite widely.

It is important for prophetically oriented people to learn to rest, recreate and have some things going on in their lives that provide a holy distraction from all the heavy issues toward which they tend to gravitate. Even God rested. The attitude with which they share their revelations with others should reveal that they may not have a perfect understanding of what needs to be done with the information. There is a time for intensity, but if it's the only "gear" in which someone operates, it paradoxically undermines their ability to be taken seriously by others. Such intensity inside a person often only comes from a need to be needed and an unsatisfied drive to be "important" in the eyes of others.

FLIPPANCY WITH HOLY THINGS

There is an opposite problem that can be just as disturbing as the above. Some people try so hard not to be intense that they become improperly loose in their language and demeanor when involved in ministering. I

115

believe that God often speaks through prophecy in riddles, word plays and with a winsome and wholesome humor. But the danger for some is that they become so familiar with the presence and gifts of God that they go overboard and become flippant with holy things.

> Then Nadab and Abihu, the sons of Aaron, each took his censer and put fire in it, put incense on it, and offered profane fire before the LORD, which He had not commanded them. So fire went out from the LORD and devoured them, and they died before the LORD. And Moses said to Aaron, "This is what the LORD spoke, saying: 'By those who come near Me I must be regarded as holy; and before all the people I must be glorified.'" So Aaron held his peace.
>
> —LEVITICUS 10:1–3

This sobering account of Nadab's and Abihu's deaths stands as a warning to us about God's attitude toward ministry. They presumptuously messed around with holy things—and treated their ministry lightly in doing so.

I always get nervous when ministers poke fun at things like the gifts of the Spirit or any other divine activity referred to in the Scriptures.

It is appropriate for us to laugh at ourselves a little, but it is inappropriate to joke and jest at the expense of the word or gifts of God. It is also unwise to become silly in our communication style when doing ministry in the name of the Lord. Sincerity in speech and conduct within a ministry setting will navigate us through the narrow channel between the rocks of "ultra-intensity" and "flippancy." Sincerity will lend a proper credibility to our prophetic ministry or any other kind of ministry.

REJECTION SYNDROME

Many people who have had genuine prophetic experiences have lived in social environments that did not understand or appreciate these kind of spiritual phenomena. As a result they have often been wounded and rejected when they tried to share and explain their experiences. The church at large has not typically been skilled at mentoring these kinds of people. As a result, a lot of these gifted members have developed eccentricities in their personalities to cope with the pain they have had in interpersonal relationships. Many have become so defensive that they expect to be misunderstood and rejected—and actually set themselves up for it to happen. Ironically, this can lead to one kind of "prophecy" that *shouldn't* be—"self-fulfilling" prophecy.

Quite a few of these believers are naturally drawn to groups that value prophetic ministry. As they land upon our congregational shores, we must seek to partner with them and help them face and overcome the relational and spiritual quirks they have adopted through the cycles of rejection and misunderstanding in their lives. With large doses of communication, validation and loving correction, they will learn to relate and function in the body in a healthy way.

Many times, and it seems surprisingly widespread, the Holy Spirit uses the image of an eagle to represent prophetic ministry. A few years back, I felt the Lord spoke this phrase to me, "Ill eagles do ill-egal things." We need a host of "eagles" throughout the body of Christ to rise and soar. My prayer is that prophets will no longer be an endangered species! It is going to take a lot of love, truth, understanding and patience between the various ministries in the whole church to see this come about. Just imagine an international host of healthy and holy prophets serving the body of Christ and touching the nations!

ECCENTRICITIES IN
DOCTRINE AND METHODOLOGY

In some church circles prophetic people have been allowed to function unchecked, often because leaders have been intimidated by their sometimes powerful gifting. This lack of accountability has allowed some to develop unbiblical ideas and ways and pass them off as normative and valid. In many cases they have become models of ministry for others to mimic.

Within constituencies of religious movements, eccentricities have become attached to the common understanding of how prophetic people are expected to conduct themselves:

- It is not necessary for them to be accountable to human leadership because they answer to God alone.

- They are given the liberty to speak dogmatically on extrabiblical issues or on nonessential matters because, supposedly, they have received a divine revelation.

- They are permitted to rebuke harshly people in public settings without following the biblical principles of confrontation.

- They may utilize manipulative and flamboyant theatrics and melodrama in their ministry style because they are really "filled with the Spirit" and are directly led to do so.

- It's OK for them to use hyperbole in their communication in order to create an atmosphere of "faith" for their gift to work.

- It's permissible for them to draw undue attention to themselves because they are the special conduits of God's power to the people.

- Ordinary believers may not approach them because they are too important and must not be distracted from their communion with God.

- They are allowed to engage in behaviors that others couldn't get away with because they are the "anointed vessels" that must never be "touched" by any criticism.

The attitude behind these eccentricities is very far indeed from the spirit of the New Testament apostles and the plain ethical injunctions of their writings. Yet many have come to associate these kinds of things with prophetic ministry. This is why the prophetic has an uphill battle to reclaim credibility in the eyes of many sincere believers who are committed to the truths and values of Scripture. The situation obviously begs for a number of healthy prophetic role models to rise up and lead the growing number of prophetic people within the body of Christ into a more excellent way.

Chapter 5

GIFTS, FRUIT
AND WISDOM

I N 1 CORINTHIANS, Paul was writing to a congregation of believers who were having many spiritual experiences, and they were obviously enthusiastic about them: "Since you are eager to have spiritual gifts, try to excel in gifts that build up the church" (1 Cor. 14:12, NIV).

Touching and being touched by the power of God through spiritual gifts can be an exhilarating experience. However, the excitement of the Corinthian believers was overruling their love and wisdom, and the expression of their gifts was becoming somewhat counterproductive to God's goal for giving them.

It is intriguing to consider that when we want to study about spiritual gifts in the church, we turn to 1 Corinthians. Yet, it is also the book we turn to when we want to expose carnality in the church! The obvious lesson is that having an abundance of gifts does not imply or secure spiritual maturity.

Paul cautions the Corinthians to discipline, temper and restrain themselves properly in order to channel their spiritual gifts in such a way that they will maximize the helpfulness of their anointings to the whole Christian community. The fourteenth verse captures the essence of Paul's pastoral burden regarding this matter. I believe that it should become the banner scripture over any group that seeks to impart and nurture prophetic ministry. Spiritual gifts are tools to help us love one another better and evangelize the lost more effectively. They are not toys to play with or badges of spirituality to flaunt. Neither are they given to us in an individualistic context, although we are individually strengthened by their proper use. Spiritual gifts find their highest use when they are seen as parts of a greater whole and ministered in coordination with the gifts of others. This is the main point of the "body analogy" Paul uses throughout 1 Corinthians.

Part of dwelling in and enjoying the "commonwealth" of the church has to do with realizing that the "whole is greater than the sum of the parts." We become significantly "richer" in the Spirit as we embrace Christian community and its necessary restraints upon our individuality, instead of isolating ourselves and trying to be spiritual "lone rangers." A godly kind of synergism is created when we mutually submit the use of our spiritual gifts for the building up of one another in the love of God.

THE BEAUTY OF TEAM MINISTRY

An "up-close-and-personal" example of this principle of mutual submission has been our leadership team here at Metro Christian Fellowship throughout the years. We have diligently sought to embrace a "team" approach to ministry.

We haven't been perfect in our understanding or application of this practice, but we have sincerely attempted to make team ministry a core value in our fellowship. Without negating the importance of recognizing specific human vessels whom God has chosen to lead specific gatherings, events or projects, we have set out to create a relational environment that allows for other leaders and church members to step into ministry situations as they are moved upon by the Lord.

Many years ago, our founding pastor, Mike Bickle, set the spiritual thermostat for the style of ministry that has developed at Metro. Undermining the "one-man show" approach to ministry was a conscious effort on his part. Scripture says that "two are better than one" (Eccles. 4:9). As a result, our fellowship of several thousand people is structured around a matrix of "ministry teams" that function on many levels. The more publicly prominent members of our leadership team really do believe in, feel and acknowledge their need for their fellow workers. This approach to ministry has actually become second nature to our leaders to the point that we hardly recognize that we are doing it. As a result, we don't talk much about it, but many believers who come to see how our fellowship works constantly refer to the unusual way that our ministers and ministry teams flow together as units. I believe that the value and practice of "team ministry" is one of the significant, yet unheralded, reasons for much of the high-impact ministry in which, by God's grace, Metro has been privileged to participate.

Another important scripture verse summarizes the main aspects of the Holy Spirit's ministry:

> For God did not give us a spirit of timidity, but a spirit of power, of love and of self-discipline.
>
> −2 TIMOTHY 1:7, NIV

I believe Paul is speaking here of the gift of the Holy Spirit in Timothy's life in contrast to a specific spiritual gift that the Spirit had imparted to Timothy. Paul didn't say, "God has given you a *gift* of power, love and discipline." Rather he said, a "spirit" of these things. This would seem to refer to the Person of the Holy Spirit Himself. He is a Spirit of power—His gifts. He is a Spirit of love—His fruit. And He is a Spirit of self-discipline—His wisdom. It is interesting to note that these three veins of the Spirit's work are each reflected in the themes of 1 Corinthians 12 (power), 13 (love) and 14 (discipline). As one surveys the Person and work of the Holy Spirit throughout the Bible, one can almost invariably see how His activity falls into one or more of these broad categories.

All three dimensions of the Spirit's ministry need to be highly valued, and we must seek to see them blended and balanced in both our individual and corporate lives. There are a number of "trinities" highlighted in the New Testament. There is faith, hope and love. There is righteousness, peace and joy. There is the Word, blood and Spirit. And of course there is the Holy Trinity—Father, Son and Holy Spirit.

Oftentimes in the symbolic language of dreams and visions, three is pictured as the "number of God." Mathematicians have described the equilateral triangle as the "strongest" geometric figure of all. A three-legged stool will never wobble, and a threefold cord is not easily broken. In reference to the Spirit's activity, any one aspect without the other two is insufficient, and likewise, any two without the other one is still deficient. It is unnecessary to exalt one dimension to the neglect of another, for the Holy Spirit is a whole Person, and He always desires to minister in the fullness of His being.

Love is to be the supreme governing principle of the church's life together in the Holy Spirit:

> Though I speak with the tongues of men and of angels, but have not love, I have become sounding brass or a clanging cymbal. And though I have the gift of prophecy, and understand all mysteries and all knowledge, and though I have all faith, so that I could remove mountains, but have not love, I am nothing. And though I bestow all my goods to feed the poor, and though I give my body to be burned, but have not love, it profits me nothing.
>
> —1 CORINTHIANS 13:1–3

In 1 Corinthians 13 we see that we can demonstrate the heights of both power (mountain-moving faith) and self-discipline (voluntary martyrdom) and yet lack the love of God as the motivation for and goal of these things. Amazingly, the apostle states that these other things have no value in God's sight unless they are intimately wedded to His love.

It seems that throughout the history of the church, groups and movements of believers have unfortunately tended to focus on one or two of these aspects of the Spirit's work and have thereby, either deliberately or inadvertently, undermined the other one or two. Some groups are the "power" folks. In their thinking, unless an observable sign or wonder occurs daily, then surely the glory of God must have departed. The Holy Spirit is viewed only as "present" if something visibly dramatic occurs. This mentality has sown seeds of religious hype and carnal exaggeration into many ministries.

Others are "into the fruit and not the gifts"—as though God expects us to choose one against the other. They just want everyone to "love one another and be happy." This bias often actually cloaks their unbelief in and fear of the power dimension of the Spirit. It can also speak of their aversion to the long-term, proper practices of the spiritual disciplines. As a result, the kind of fruit they cultivate is not of the quality that reflects the Spirit's life. They settle for humanistic "plastic fruit."

Good gardening requires much effort. God's way in human life involves our need to practice rhythmically many kinds of "humility drills" in order to cultivate the genuine fruit of the Spirit in our lives. We don't earn God's love and favor by these things. But we do posture our-selves in the ways that God has ordained for us to receive His grace—personal prayer, private giving, secret fasting, intensive study, deliberate solitude and silence, purposeful (vs. random!) acts of unannounced kindness and the like. The secret of a spiritual life is to have a secret spiritual life before our heavenly Father who "sees in secret."

Still others are into discipline as *the* way of bringing real honor to God. They have focused so much on Good Friday that they never get to the point of celebrating Resurrection Sunday! They are so much into preparation that they never get onto the playing field of actually loving and ministering to others through the power of the Spirit. There is a narcissistic kind of self-absorption that constantly distracts and paralyzes them from moving out into ministry because they are preoccupied with their own development, born out of a twisted kind of concern that everything "be just right." This is the kind of spiritual soil in which a counterfeit religious and legalistic unholy spirit flourishes among professing Christians. Things will only become "right" as we courageously embark on the journey of growing in and actively serving the Lord, and this will always include many uncertainties along the way.

I have come to observe six specific general deficiencies (two sets of three) that are generated in both individuals or groups by the lack of the presence of all three dimensions and emphases of the Spirit's work and personality.

1. Power without love or discipline—triumphalism and hype
2. Love without discipline or power—humanism or spiritual fantasy
3. Discipline without power or love—legalism

The expressions of the next set are not quite as unhealthy as those above, but they are still significantly problematic.

1. Power and love without discipline—disorder and stagnancy
2. Love and discipline without power—spiritual boredom
3. Discipline and power without love—performance orientation

A classic demonic strategy must be preying upon the human tendency to confine, control and boast in our strengths, and it has led to these caricatures of New

Testament Christianity. I believe that the Lord Jesus is working in our day to bring together all the streams of the Holy Spirit's ministry into a unified river as the end of the age comes upon the earth. By the grace of God, the church of Jesus Christ is going to get her act together before a watching and longing world. The unbelieving world is inaudibly crying out for the church to be the church, although most unbelievers would never admit it. This fullness of the Spirit manifested in the body of Christ will result in the greatest evangelistic harvest in the history of the world. The unreached multitudes of this generation will get the best opportunity to believe in Jesus that the world has ever known.

Unprecedented power demonstrations through the body, unparalleled unity and love within the body and unknown degrees of widespread self-sacrifice among the members of the body are going to characterize the church of the twenty-first millennium. However, it won't occur without the release of significant, temporal and global divine judgments that will stimulate both the church and the world to respond in faith. My spiritual father in the prophetic ministry, Paul Cain, has prophesied, "There will be a rude awakening before there will be a great awakening." Already these events are happening in the earth in a preliminary measure. I believe that shocking world news will continue to reach our ears, touch our nations and intensify in their magnitude and frequency until Christ returns. The earth has begun a time of "transitional labor" that will bring to birth the fullness of the kingdom of God and the end of this age.

> With my soul I have desired You in the night, yes, by
> my spirit within me I will seek You early; for when

Your judgments are in the earth, the inhabitants of the world will learn righteousness.

—ISAIAH 26:9

And you will hear of wars and rumors of wars. See that you are not troubled; for all these things must come to pass, but the end is not yet. For nation will rise against nation, and kingdom against kingdom. And there will be famines, pestilences, and earthquakes in various places. All these are the beginning of sorrows....And this gospel of the kingdom will be preached in all the world as a witness to all the nations, and then the end will come.

—MATTHEW 24:6–8, 14

REACHING FOR FULLNESS

Pursue love, and desire spiritual gifts, but especially that you may prophesy.

—1 CORINTHIANS 14:1

When it comes to the ministry of prophecy, all three of these elements—gifts, fruit and wisdom—come into play. Of course, love and the building up of others is to be our ultimate motivation and aim in the use of the prophetic ministry. However, we must also obey the apostolic command to desire the prophetic ministry of the Spirit. We can love people even better with the power of the Spirit in operation.

The supernatural power of the gift itself can profoundly penetrate the human heart to impart conviction and faith.

But if all prophesy, and an unbeliever or an unin-
formed person comes in, he is convinced by all, he is
convicted by all. And thus the secrets of his heart are
revealed; and so, falling down on his face, he will
worship God and report that God is truly among you.
                                    —1 CORINTHIANS 14:24–25

On a few occasions I have been blessed to see this
kind of "power evangelism" working through my life and
ministry. On one recent occasion during our corporate
worship service, the Spirit impressed me that a particular
man I had never before met or seen in our fellowship
meeting was going to receive Jesus as his Savior that very
morning. I also was led to go to the microphone and
actually call this man out of the crowd. I boldly proclaimed that God was *at that very moment* calling this
man to become a disciple of Jesus Christ and that the
Spirit was showing me that God was washing away all his
past sins. I declared that God was making him into a new
creature in Christ. I then asked him to wave at our whole
fellowship if he wanted to publicly acknowledge Jesus as
his Lord for the first time in his life. He did so, and a
wave of joy and cheering went across our assembly.

I then prophesied that the Holy Spirit had spoken to
my heart that this man was just a token of the changed
lives we will see through the release of prophetic evangelism in the coming days. I have to admit that after the
conscious anointing of the Spirit lifted from me, I was
somewhat anxious as to what had actually transpired!

A few days later, my good friend and fellow pastor
Kirk Bennett told me he had spoken to this man in depth.
He reported to Kirk that just moments before I had
pointed him out, he had silently prayed for Christ to

come into his life for the first time. A true miracle had occurred in the presence of our whole congregation. Of course, all the glory for this salvation belongs to the Lord, but He does delight to use human instruments in the work of His kingdom. I am constantly amazed to the point of wonderment over this reality. I am not sure that there is a greater feeling in this world than to know that God has worked miraculously through us despite our human frailties.

DISCIPLINE AND THE USE OF PROPHECY

It is very important to understand that placing necessary limits on the public use of prophecy and scrutinizing revelatory claims will not quench the Holy Spirit. In fact, God's Word mandates these measures.

> Two or three prophets should speak, and the others should weigh carefully what is said. And if a revelation comes to someone who is sitting down, the first speaker should stop. For you can all prophesy in turn so that everyone may be instructed and encouraged. The spirits of prophets are subject to the control of prophets. For God is not a God of disorder but of peace.
> —1 CORINTHIANS 14:29–33, NIV

> Do not put out the Spirit's fire; do not treat prophecies with contempt. Test everything. Hold on to the good.
> —1 THESSALONIANS 5:19–21, NIV

The Holy Spirit is very secure in His Personhood, and He understands our need to examine carefully the things that people claim He has inspired them to say and do. In fact, He is the one who has commanded us to do so! True revelation from the Holy Spirit can stand up to this kind of evaluation process.

It is this third aspect of establishing boundaries and applying self-restraint in the use of prophecy that many prophetic people don't appreciate and often chafe against. Actually, these disciplines are for the protection not only of the rest of the body, but for the prophetic people themselves. Parents put fences around their yards so that their children can safely play without endangering themselves. Within those loving boundaries, there is great security and liberty. Without them, true liberty is threatened.

In the midst of cataloging the supernatural manifestations and ministries within the church in 1 Corinthians 12:28, Paul speaks of the charismatic gift of *administrations*. In the Greek language, this word was used of one who steered a vessel. Church governors are ordained by God and gifted by the Spirit Himself to govern and administrate wisely the use of prophecy and other spiritual gifts within the body to ensure that they all work together to further the overall purposes of God. Prophetic people should walk in proper submission to fellow church members and leaders in the use of their individual gifting. There is a "prophetic etiquette" that needs to be taught and learned in the Lord's house so that the gift of prophecy can be utilized to its fullest intent and extent.

FOUR GOVERNING VALUES— ### LOVE, INTEGRITY, HUMILITY AND PASSIONATE PURSUIT

I have identified four basic values that will make prophecy more helpful if embraced. I am certain there are others

131

that could be added to the list. Actually, these values do not apply only to prophecy, but also to any ministry in the body of Christ. However, I will seek to apply them more specifically to the prophetic arena. *Adopting values and holding them in our hearts has an "informing effect" upon us.* The difficult and confusing questions that surface as we attempt to practice a given thing bring wisdom as we ponder the implications of the basic values that govern that practice. Maybe you are facing something very practical and specific that you have never faced before. If your basic values are in place, they will help inform you about the course you should take.

Chapter 6

WHAT DOES
LOVE IMPLY?

PEOPLE HAVE BOTH *heightened fears and hopes* when they are exposed to the potential of receiving prophetic ministry. They are afraid of having their sins, failures or weaknesses exposed—especially in front of other people. They are afraid of missing something that God might really want to say to them through another person. They are afraid of being deceived or manipulated by a supposed word from the Lord. Then again, they are hopeful that God will put His finger on sins, failures and weaknesses because they really do want His evaluation of their lives. They are also hopeful that a prophecy might confirm and affirm their giftings, callings and some of the magnificent personal promises that they believe He has given to them in the past.

These dynamics put sincere believers in a vulnerable posture. Some prophetic people are very aware of this personal and social tension, and they "play it" to their own

133

advantage. Usually they do this in order to bolster their sense of self-importance. Sometimes they do it for worse reasons. But these carnal motivations are dishonoring to the Holy Spirit and to the people of God. Those who minister the gift of prophecy must purpose in their hearts not to take advantage of their brothers and sisters in Christ who are hungry to receive a genuine word from God.

An apparently true story is told about a fellow who viewed himself as some sort of a prophet. He had been very disappointed with his local church for some reason, and at a certain point his patience had apparently run out. On one particular day when the fellowship had gathered, he made his way to the front and managed to commandeer a microphone. He was well versed in the Old Testament prophetic literature and very eloquently began to castigate the church *a la* Jeremiah and Ezekiel for quite a few minutes. At the crescendo of his scathing rebuke, he forcefully proclaimed—"And the Lord God saith unto this people that they are rejected of Me, for they are a rebellious house. Yea, verily, I have even written over this house 'Michelob' (a well-known brand of beer!), for surely the glory of thy God has departed." Of course, he meant to say "Ichabod," but his misspeaking served to put the whole event into perspective!

Many people have gotten it into their heads that angry and frustrated members of the body who view everything dogmatically gravitate to prophetic ministry. In fact, many truly prophetically oriented people *have* become angry, and they soak themselves in the corrective messages to ancient Israel by the prophets of God. They fancy the church of the Lord Jesus to be parallel to Israel in its seasons of unfaithfulness and apostasy. They irresponsibly apply God's stern Old Testament warnings and rebukes to backslidden Israel to their fellow believers in Christ.

However, this picture is a far cry from the New Testament use of the gift of prophecy. In the Old Testament there were many occasions in which God reluctantly found Himself in an adversarial relationship with His people. He did raise up prophets as His voice to herald coming judgments. However, in the New Testament all believers have the Spirit, and the prophets among them are *in partnership* with the whole body in discerning and bringing forth the word of God. The church is prophetic in its very essence. Through the church, God answered the sigh of Moses in Numbers 11:29: "Oh, that all the LORD's people were prophets and that the LORD would put His Spirit upon them!" Any member of the body is potentially prophetic, for the Spirit indwells each of them. This implies that there is a kind of mutual submission and accountability regarding prophetic ministry among the New Testament people of God that is absent in the Old Testament function of the prophetic.

In the New Testament, the church is the bride of Christ—believers are the friends and children of God. The whole relational context and paradigm is qualitatively different from God's relationship to Israel in the Old Testament. Those who minister prophetically to the church do well to remember the differences. When we prophesy to the church, we are addressing those beloved of God for Christ's sake, and whatever failures are present, they have not brought the wrath of God down upon the whole church. The work of Jesus Christ really has made a difference in God's relationship to and fellowship with His people! Surely, there is an appropriate time for New Testament-type prophetic ministry to bring correction and even rebuke, but the foundation from which it issues forth is in the spirit of an advocate rather than that of an adversary.

DEALING WITH "HEAVY" PROPHECY

I believe in the validity of "mystical" Christian experiences. Paul and Peter both fell into trances. Paul was caught up into the third heaven and shown things about which he wasn't permitted to speak. (Another thing that some prophetic people need to consider!) God speaks directly to people through angels, voices and visitations. The mystics of church history who didn't spin off into error focused on love, intimacy, submission, patience, joy, suffering and humility. Their experiences were full of these kinds of things, and their prophetic messages were built around them.

This leads to some important qualifications in ministering the gift of prophecy. Many words of valid New Testament-type prophecy do not require any particular response from the people on the receiving end of them. They simply make their positive impact. If it is a personal prophecy, the person who receives the word goes his way encouraged and edified, since it bears witness to him for any variety of reasons. Likewise, if it is a corporate word, the church in general feels the positive impact—it just "goes down well," and everyone knows and feels it. No one really has to "judge" it beyond this. We have an advantage in regard to judging prophetic utterances over the first-century church—and even present-day believers (as in China) who do not have many Bibles—because we have the canon of Scripture. And most believers are fairly familiar with basic Christian doctrines.

Related to the subject of judging utterances, I have

envisaged a small flag and a flagpole within every Spirit-filled member of the church. When a true prophetic word is released to a congregation, it is as though that little flag quickly runs up the pole and begins to wave with joyous energy within the spirits of virtually every member. This represents the operation of the internal witness of the Holy Spirit in believers who are present when a true "word from the Lord" comes forth in public. Usually, we can all tell when this happens because we hear and enjoy the "oohs," "ahhs" and "amens" coming from our brothers and sisters.

However, there are three categories of prophecy that are more inherently difficult to deal with, and special care must be taken to guard against the abuse of such prophecy. The first is *predictive* prophecy. The second is *directive* prophecy. The third is *corrective* prophecy. Each type must be examined as it applies to both personal and corporate prophecies.

PREDICTIVE PROPHECY

Pure predictive prophecy is actually the easiest of the three to handle. Many times God prophetically reveals an aspect of the future so that when a person or a group comes to the time when it is fulfilled, they are strengthened in their faith. From that point they move ahead in God's purposes with a greater confidence that God is really with them. Often it implies that their faith will be severely tested, and the fulfilled prophecy stabilizes them on their journey. If such a word doesn't come to pass, then one of two things is true. The first possibility is that the conditions for the word coming to pass weren't met. (It could also be that the conditions for it to be avoided have been met—as with Jonah and Ninevah.) Many times these conditions are overlooked on the front end of such a prophecy.

The second possibility is that it was an errant word. If someone gives an errant predictive prophecy, his or her credibility has to be reexamined. It could be that they simply spoke out of their own heart or mind.

> Thus says the LORD of hosts: "Do not listen to the words of the prophets who prophesy to you. They make you worthless; they speak a vision of their own heart, not from the mouth of the LORD."
>
> —JEREMIAH 23:16

Many sincere believers have done this kind of thing before and lived to tell the story! This doesn't automatically make them a "false prophet" in the classic sense. It's really hard to be a "true Christian" and a "false prophet" at the same time! If such an errant utterance has been given publicly, then some kind of public statement needs to be made to clear up the matter. If it was given privately, then public exposure would not be necessary. Whatever the case, wrong predictive "prophecies" need to be accounted for in a proper way. We encourage our members to submit any corporate predictive prophecies to the pastoral leadership in private before any public utterances are given.

Real false prophets are usually many years and deceptions in the making. However, there are real false prophets who are in league with the evil one and deluded by evil spirits. Telling the difference between a mistaken Christian and a false prophet is usually not too challenging, given a little bit of time. There are many examples in the history of the church of people who were viewed and received as genuine anointed leaders among believers who later turned away from loving the truth and serving the Lord in purity. They did indeed become false prophets and teachers. Peter and Jude warned the churches of their day about such deceivers who were trying to sneak into the Christian community. (See 2 Peter 2 and the Book of Jude.) This warning is no less true today.

Although it is difficult to be a "true Christian" and a "false prophet" at the same time, there may be people who at least appear to be true prophets and teachers who clearly become false prophets and teachers. In a firsthand way, I have, on occasion, witnessed this kind of fall happen quite quickly.

One of the great mysteries of God's ways is how people who have "gone bad" or will "go bad" in either heart or doctrine can move in power ministry among God's people. In my mind, Judas Iscariot stands as the preeminent New Testament example of this paradox. He was chosen by Jesus and walked with Him and the other eleven apostles in power ministry for several years.

> Jesus answered them, "Did I not choose you, the twelve, and one of you is a devil?" He spoke of Judas Iscariot, the son of Simon, for it was he who would betray Him, being one of the twelve.
> —JOHN 6:70–71

True ministry in the Holy Spirit is not just about supernatural information or power. It is primarily about cultivating and maintaining an intimate and faithful relationship with God and His words of truth. One of the philosophical tensions we face and will face as we move into prophetic ministry will be that prophecy, on one hand, is a free gift that cannot be earned. However, we need to know that we will never see the fullness of the divine purpose for which God has entrusted to us this giftedness unless we focus upon cultivating an intimate friendship with the Holy Trinity and subordinate the use of our gifts to this end. Those of us who are hungry for the prophetic need to heed this sober warning:

> Many will say to Me in that day, "Lord, Lord, have we not prophesied in Your name, cast out demons in Your name, and done many wonders in Your name?" And then I will declare to them, "I never knew you; depart from Me, you who practice lawlessness!"
> —MATTHEW 7:22–23

I recently had an experience in which I received and communicated a predictive prophecy. In the midst of a quite severe drought here in Kansas City this last summer, the Lord revealed to me that He was (most likely among many other things) utilizing it as a sign of His displeasure over a situation that was confronting our leadership. The unrelenting 100-degree heat and the lack of rain meant that He was putting loving pressure upon us to bring a godly verbal correction to bear upon and to apply biblical discipline to this situation. He spoke to my heart that on whatever day we arranged this encounter, He was immediately afterward going to send a rain shower as an indicator of His relenting mercy toward us and our ministry.

I decided to e-mail this predictive word to all of our governmental leaders both to go on record and to be accountable to them for my words. It would have been unnecessary and inappropriate to release this word in a public forum. About four or five days later, this confrontation took place. I had no control over the timing of this meeting and wasn't even called to be a part of it. I also had no knowledge of the weather predictions, and as far as I know, rain was not even expected on that day. However, a few hours later, after a cloudless day, an intense rainstorm hit the Kansas City area—with a lot of thunder and lightning thrown in to boot! I knew that our leaders had pleased the Lord in this difficult assignment. More importantly, they knew that they were standing on the Lord's ground in a situation that was fraught with much spiritual warfare, confusion and deceit. That was the end of the 100-degree weather, and more rain did fall on our area in that last part of the summer.

God will often establish a prophetic person in the eyes of the church and church leaders by the fulfillment of predictive prophecies. As their "track record" of accuracy is validated, their words need to be taken more seriously. Where predictive prophecy becomes more challenging than ever is when it is linked with the next type—directive prophecy.

DIRECTIVE PROPHECY

It's one thing to have the luxury to wait and see if a predictive prophecy will come to pass or not. It's totally another thing when the prophecy contains elements that require some kind of action or response in the present—"The Lord is saying that if we will do (or not do) a certain thing, then He will do (or not do) this specific thing." When the actions or lack of them is outside the realm of clear biblical commands, then the church (or individual in the case of a personal prophecy) is faced with a thorny decision. It is also possible that there would be no predictive element in the prophecy, but simply a declaration—"The Lord says do this or that." The church is still on the spot to evaluate and respond to such a word. This is what I mean by *directive prophecy*.

More than once I have been in a gathering in which someone boldly declared, "Take off your shoes, for the ground you are on is holy ground." (I hate it when that happens!) In my earlier days of leadership I would dutifully start taking my shoes off, and all the others, with their eyes fixed upon me, would reluctantly follow suit. These days, I would probably "stand my ground" (no pun intended) and try kindly to reinterpret the word somehow. That is, unless it was a *real* prophecy, and then I'd expect that the whole congregation would know the difference. Sometimes people say things in the name of the Lord that forces the church and its leadership to make a "judgment call" on the spot, and I have rarely seen this dynamic to be edifying to the church or to the person who gave the word.

I believe that God can and does direct His people through prophecy. Joseph and Mary were guided by it. Paul was also in his missionary endeavors. It's just that it is "heavy" by nature, and special precautions are unfortunately required—especially when it doesn't come directly to you, but rather through another person who claims that God has spoken to them about you! Many people and churches have allowed prophecy to guide them without any confirming internal witness of the Holy Spirit or some unrelated unsolicited sources of confirmation attending it. This has caused untold heartache in many people in the history of prophetic movements within the church.

Classic examples of this often revolve around marriages. I knew a pastor and his wife who had married each other

142

based upon a supposed "prophecy" from someone within their fellowship. They apparently had no romantic attraction to one another and didn't share many things in common outside of their faith in Jesus. They felt obligated to "obey the Lord" and get married. In the years that followed, they realized that this had been an abuse of prophecy and felt embarrassed about how they had come together. It got to the point where it seemed to them that they had made an unrecoverable mistake "in the beginning," and that they had "married outside of God's will." After this oppressive mind-set had worked upon them for a number of years, their marriage became so unbearable that they divorced. All this confusion flowed out of the trauma of a false utterance. Apparently, there are many such horror stories within the body of Christ.

In our training and mentoring of the prophetic in our midst, we have taught people to walk very carefully in the arenas of romance, childbirths and money matters. Unless there is a specific miracle of some kind that God intends to predict and perform, then, in our view, these matters should be avoided by prophetic ministers. An abundance of fleshly "words" have been given out in these arenas and have soiled the use and reputation of prophecy in the body of Christ.

Usually prophecy functions in a *confirming* role for a direction that God has already communicated to a person or a group through other means. If it is used in giving direction, then it is appropriate to ask the Lord for another witness of some kind to confirm that decision. In our fellowship we have asked our members to submit directional words for the church to the pastoral leadership in advance for evaluation and to help determine a proper application. If the members of the church trust that their leaders are seeking to be sensitive to the Lord and obedient to the Holy Spirit, then this method does not pose a problem. If the members of the church don't trust their leaders, then there are bigger problems present than discerning a single prophecy!

CORRECTIVE PROPHECY

Prophecies that are correctional in nature are similar to directional ones. I don't think the Lord expects us to submit to a correction to which we ultimately don't bear witness within ourselves. This does not ensure that we don't need the correction, and we should open our hearts to the Lord and some trusted friends to avoid deceiving ourselves. When the Lord has gently and firmly corrected me or our fellowship through a prophetic word, there has always been an inner knowing that it was a true word— even though it cut deeply. The awareness of the presence of God typically attends such dealings and disciplines. There is a "tonal quality" that is unique to the voice of our Father in heaven, which distinguishes it from every other voice in the universe. The more we immerse ourselves in prayerful meditation upon the Scriptures, the more easily and frequently we will "hear" it.

If someone believes he or she has received a negative revelation about another person, special care must be taken to steward it properly. The following steps should be followed carefully:

1. Discipline should not be administered on the basis of a subjective revelation. God expects us to take such heavy action on the basis of verified facts.

144

2.   God may have revealed the problem for the purpose of inspiring intercession on behalf of that person. You can't go wrong praying for the individual, whatever the case. Praying for others helps to get us in the right frame of spirit to be most loving to others.

3.   It is advisable to wait for the right time to approach a person to ask about the specific issue. When you do approach, asking questions rather than leveling accusations is the appropriate way to respond. It may not even be necessary to speak of the revelation you have received.

4.   If you are doubting whether to speak with someone along these lines, ask the Lord to set up a situation that will convince you that it is the appropriate time.

5.   It is sometimes necessary or wise to get counsel from a third party without exposing the person who may have the problem.

The bottom line is that we want to serve people with any genuine prophetic insight we receive from God, and we want to share that insight in the timing and way that gives the best chance for receiving it.

Recently I had a clear impression to bring a word of adjustment to a friend over a situation in a relationship. I prayed for just the right opportunity to arise and that I would know it when it came. A few of days later I happened to run into him in an unexpected private setting. I knew this was the time and place to speak up, and I silently prayed for wisdom. God had great mercy upon me. This fellow happens to be a real seeker of the Lord—and a prophetically gifted person as well. The first words that came out of his mouth after we greeted was, "Hey Michael, I had a dream last night about us. Actually, you were bringing me a correction about being too critical toward others."

That was the very issue that I needed to address with him. All I could do was smile as I gently told him the specific relational situation that I felt he needed to address. I gave him a few new insights and some pointers, and that was it. He promptly went out that week and addressed the issue in a loving and humble way, bringing it to a sweet resolution. The Holy Spirit is such a marvelous Person, and so is my dear friend. By the way, it goes without saying that it doesn't always work this way!

PROPERLY HONORING AUTHORITY

Just as there certainly is a realm of prophetic authority, there are other spheres of God-ordained authority that must be honored by those who minister in this gift. The authority of church leaders and the authority of each individual person must be honored. Prophetic people are obligated to package their words in a way that gives others the proper "space" to which they are entitled when it comes to receiving and evaluating prophecy. This can be done by carefully using language that is respectful, well qualified and less authoritative when touching the realms of prediction, direction and correction. In the case of corporate words, it can be accomplished by submitting such words to the appointed leadership before they are uttered in public. This is especially true in the early stages of a person's prophetic ministry. When speaking prophetically, it is important for them also to give "easy outs" to others by using gracious words and a nonauthoritative style of communicating. In this way the persons receiving the prophecy aren't forced to distance themselves from the person who is delivering the word, even if they can't at that time receive the prophetic word. In my view, this is not compromising or watering down the word of God—it is showing proper love and respect to others. Genuine prophecy will still make its impact even if the style of delivery is "dialed down." Those who become mature and proven in prophetic ministry will, over the course of time, naturally be given more liberty by the Spirit and the body to express themselves more boldly and confidently.

The method of privately submitting predictive, directional and correctional prophecies to church leadership is rooted in two basic convictions. First, if the Lord really has a significant new direction or correction for any particular person or group, it will probably be true next week and next month as well as today. This reality typically provides time, which enables the involved parties to weigh the words patiently and pray over these kinds of heavier words.

Second, direction and correction officially fall within the biblical job description of the governors of the church. True, God may speak such through any member of the body by the spirit of prophecy, but ultimately it must be evaluated and ratified by the duly appointed pastoral leaders of the fellowship of believers. Genuine direction and correction from the Holy Spirit will best be established in the life of the church through the voice of their leadership anyway—even though the leadership may not be the original source of the information or wisdom.

It needs to be noted that special attention will be given naturally by the leadership to those whom God has established in proven prophetic ministry over the course of time and through many experiences. Newcomers and those with no prophetic history upon which to draw need to appreciate this reality and wait on God to establish them in their new church context.

If we expect to be utilized by the Lord in whatever spiritual gifts we have been given, we must be joined to the local body and submitted to its spiritual leadership. This is especially true of prophetic ministry. Otherwise, we cannot expect people to let down their guard to receive words that carry such potential weight from total strangers and independent types. Too often we see prophetic-type people roaming around the body of Christ, trying to find a group of people to give them instant credibility in their ministry. It just won't happen—and it's not supposed to. Anyone who desires long-term credibility in ministry needs to embrace the built-in checks and balances that are a part of local church life. It's good for our souls!

Chapter 7

WHAT DOES INTEGRITY DEMAND?

U NFORTUNATELY, IN THE minds of many sincere believers, prophetic ministry has become somewhat notorious for a lack of integrity. They have witnessed leaders and others bend some of the "rules" by which everyone else is expected to live and minister, just so they do not offend some prophetic person who supposedly has a special "hot line" to God. This dynamic is especially powerful when pastoral leaders or a particular church are first exposed to prophetic power. The thought of challenging or correcting the person through whom that power comes is rather intimidating.

However, if we refuse to deal honestly with problems in prophetic ministry, we are setting the stage for prophetic ministry ultimately to be despised and discredited altogether. Unless human failures that may attend it are acknowledged and accounted for, there will be a slow erosion of confidence regarding the blessings of prophecy in the hearts of sincere believers who previously opened themselves up to it. There are several typical arenas where the integrity principle needs to be applied to the prophetic.

SOUND THEOLOGY

First there is the arena of Scripture and theology. Many prophetically gifted people, like many other members in the body of Christ, have not been well-trained in theological matters. Yet, because of their genuine anointing and verbal skills, some of them become influential leaders in the church world. Spiritually hungry believers often take their teachings and the theological implications of their prophecies very seriously without realizing that these leaders have interpreted some of the prophetic illumination they have received through the lenses of their own theological understanding (or misunderstanding!).

Many prophetically gifted people have had experiences in which God has spoken to them through the Bible in a mystical way. God is certainly capable of doing that. The Bible is supernaturally "sophisticated"—who can know all of the levels and possible applications of its divine inspiration? God is a literary genius of the highest order! Even biblical prophecy itself confirms this point.

Many of the prophetic passages in the Bible are like the transparent overlays often used in encyclopedias to show the different systems of the human body. One page shows the skeletal system. The next page shows the vital organs. The next reveals the muscular system. And so on. Each page reveals more without obscuring or negating what was revealed on the previous pages. Old Testament prophecies often have two, three or even four valid fulfillments or theological applications. They have a historical/cultural ful-fillment and application. They may also have a Messianic fulfillment. They often have an application for the early church or for the church in general. And finally, they may have an eschatological/global fulfillment.

Scriptures may take on a very personal application by God's providence. The Holy Spirit can lead people to cer-tain passages, pull them out of their historical/cultural context and apply it to a contemporary situation without "batting an eye." Many of the inspired writers of the New Testament received a contemporary "prophetic" applica-tion to Old Testament passages and prophecies. These applications applied not only to the writer personally, but to the whole church.

Thousands of Christians have testified to this kind of experience with the Lord. However, if these experiences are frequent, then it is easy for these people to believe that is the normative way (or the "best" way—God forbid!) to discover truth from the Scriptures. Prophecy—and its applications—should never be viewed as a substitute for the more objective principles of Scripture study and interpretation. Neither should these experiences be used to establish essential doctrines of the church—although they may confirm and illumine them.

When people do give contemporary prophetic applica-tions to Bible passages, their experience becomes much more credible if they acknowledge that their use of the passage is not its primary or fundamental use. Explaining the original intent of the author will validate subjective experience, and it should always be subjected to the scrutiny of more objective truth and methodology. Objective truth is the foundation for subjective experience.

A subjective approach to the Bible, left to itself, lacks the disciplined thought and study that it takes to become truly theologically informed. It will seriously undermine the wonderful contributions of hundreds of thoughtful, believing theologians that God has given to the church throughout the centuries if it becomes wrongly exalted as "the right method." Some of the strangest doctrines and concepts have blown like winds through the body of Christ, taken out of the context of prophetic-type people with a genuine anointing from God who received new "revelation," found a public platform and preached it with strong conviction. As a result, seeds of error and division have been sown in the church throughout history. Some of these aberrant ideas have grown up into full-blown heresies. Sadly, this scenario is being repeated in our own day.

MISAPPLYING GENUINE EXPERIENCES

Many times genuine prophetic experiences have been misinterpreted and/or misapplied because they were not "pulled though the grid" of orthodox theology in the process of stewarding the experience. This is one of the most important reasons why prophetic people need to function in the context of healthy church life where theologically minded teachers and leaders are also present. I'm not suggesting that prophetic people are unable to be theologically wise, but it seems that many of them have not been gifted by God to be oriented this way. Maybe this reflects a "larger design" by the Lord to inspire interdependence within the church between the teachers and the prophets! They really do need each other, just as the church as a whole needs them both. This was reflected in the church at Antioch, out of which came the first missionary journey of Paul and Barnabas, which changed the course of human history. What might happen in our day if prophets and teachers get together?

> Now in the church that was at Antioch there were certain prophets and teachers: Barnabas, Simeon who was called Niger, Lucius of Cyrene, Manaen who had been brought up with Herod the tetrarch, and Saul. As they ministered to the Lord and fasted, the Holy Spirit said, "Now separate to Me Barnabas and Saul for the work to which I have called them." Then, having fasted and prayed, and laid hands on them, they sent them away.
>
> —ACTS 13:1–3

Prophetic experiences and ministry need to be made subject to the essentials of well-established orthodox, evangelical theology. When "prophetic words" are spoken that run counter to it, they need to be reexamined, reinterpreted and reapplied by the body of Christ. Pastoral leaders need to have the courage to call to account both prophetic people and words that don't line up with sound doctrine. Those who have misspoken need to have the integrity to acknowledge the nature of the error of which they have been convicted and make it right in the appropriate context by the appropriate method.

CORRECTING ERRORS AND CLEANING UP MISTAKES

This naturally leads to the next point in which integrity must be applied to prophetic ministry. We must have the willingness to "clean up" any mistakes or errors that occur in the exercising of prophecy. This is the only way to maintain a clear "corporate conscience" regarding prophecy in general. Paul cautioned the Thessalonians not to "despise prophecies" (1 Thess. 5:19).

At first glance, this seems like a strange temptation for a first-century church to fall into. But they must have learned quickly, as many have today, that this ministry is not an exact science. It is normative for the fallible "human factor" to enter the picture and muddy the waters. Maybe the Thessalonians had allowed spurious prophecies to go unchecked, and they slowly and silently began to despise the genuine gift. Maybe they had some eccentric prophetic-type members who had been allowed to take too much liberty in an earlier season, and now they were overreacting. Most likely, the primary source of the complicating problems with prophecy was not the presence of demonically deceived people who had sneaked into their community of believers. Rather, like today, it was more often sincere believers in Christ who would, from time to time, confuse impressions from their own imaginations, minds and hearts with the inspiration of the Holy Spirit.

When people seek to obey the spirit of Paul's admonition to earnestly desire prophecy, and when the body of believers around them are encouraging the use of this spiritual gift, there will inevitably be occasions when people will make "honest" mistakes in the process of learning to prophesy. Their primary motivation will be to please the Lord and help others. They are not deliberately trying to deceive people by passing off their own thoughts as the "mind of the Lord." This reality should not shock or scandalize us. Rather, we should be prepared to handle it wisely when it occurs.

Part of maturing in prophetic ministry in the church is akin to toddlers tripping and falling as they learn to walk. Parents do not chastise them for these mishaps. They watch with pleasure as their little ones are growing up. Yet, they do seek to protect their children from injury by allowing them to learn only under their supervision and in the environment chosen by the parents. Parents learn quickly that they have to "toddler-proof" their home to protect it from injury! They soon discover the value of the word *no* in this process as well! Parents overcome any fear of hurting their child's feelings in order to achieve more necessary and important ends. Children learn to take loving correction and benefit by it.

Pastoral leaders should seek to provide the right environment for believers to learn to move in prophecy. They need to find the balance between granting liberties and enforcing restraints. They also need to discern the different kinds and degrees of potential mistakes and respond appropriately when people do err. They need to balance encouraging individuals to step out in faith to prophesy with protecting others from the fallout of mistakes that happen as those individuals seek to minister. They need to guard against overreacting when mistakes are made so that people do not become paralyzed from taking the necessary risks associated with learning to prophesy. This is obviously a pretty significant challenge for pastoral leaders.

Three Types of Spurious "Prophecy"

Sometimes in our zeal for integrity we become impatient and unnecessarily hard on people. This can easily happen when bringing correction to the prophetic in the church. One of the ways we can guard against this is by discerning the different categories of spurious prophetic words that may occur in a church and the distinct responses that are called for. When reflecting on this issue, I think of the analogy of eating food and how our physical digestive system reacts to it. The spiritual body—the church—eats spiritual food; it also possesses a type of spiritual digestive system. Genuine prophecy is a healthy and nutritious spiritual food, and spurious "prophecy" is nonhealthy—sometimes toxic—spiritual "food." I will apply the analogy to three different general types of spurious "prophecy."

The first and easiest type of problem "prophecy" to deal with is the simply *unanointed* kind. These words might be compared to some of the "filler" found in some foods that have no nutritional value but that pass through our digestive systems without causing any real trouble. A loving local church should have a fairly high tolerance level for immature people sharing words that don't seem to really hit the mark. These words don't contain doctrinal errors or strange demands, but they also don't carry the power to impact individuals or the body spiritually. When these kinds of words are spoken, people may yawn, frown or smile a little, but they do no real damage.

If a person becomes prone to speaking out these kinds of words, especially in public gatherings, that person should be approached gently and informed as to how he or she is coming across to others. That person needs to be coached as to when it is appropriate to speak in the future and when it is not. Care should be taken to avoid discouraging the individual, and he or she should be affirmed for trying to speak out what the Lord was giving.

A second type of spurious "prophecy" is one that contains *errors* that flow out of the human heart or mind. Sincere believers are quite capable of this kind of thing, and although they need to be corrected, they must not be labeled as "false prophets." These kinds of words can cause various degrees of spiritual indigestion in the body, depending upon the nature and significance of the errors. If this happens in a public service and the errors are blatant, pastoral leaders may need to gently address the issue and offer to speak with the person afterward. These kinds of words evoke a "groan" out of the members of the body when they occur.

A third type of erroneous "prophecy" is the variety based in people being *deceived by evil spirits* to varying degrees. Sometimes they are weak pawns who are being manipulated by the evil one. At other times, they are his willing servants. These kinds of words are like ingesting poison into the body. Firm and decisive action must be taken in these instances to bring immediate correction. Again, a gentle and calm spirit should generally be maintained by the authorities of the church in the means by which the correction is given. A healthy body of believers vomits out such words even as they are being spoken. People's spiritual "red lights" start flashing as many of them immediately discern the evil source of such words. The church should not tolerate such "prophetic words" just out of sympathy for the person who is being deceived.

Of course, I have not dealt with every possible kind of erroneous prophecy or comprehensively covered all the possible responses that a church might be required to take. Hopefully, just encouraging people to think in the different categories will lead them to ask for and receive divine wisdom for any specific situation that may arise in the future. A right diagnosis of any problem will serve to yield a right prescription.

Chapter 8

WHAT DOES HUMILITY LOOK LIKE?

THE MORE YEARS I live in the kingdom of God, the more convinced I become of the importance of believers learning the ways of humility before God and man. A spirit of humility will preserve a prophetic person or group from many unnecessary trials and errors. But there are a few misconceptions about humility that need to be addressed before we proceed to apply it to the practice of prophecy.

Let me begin by stating what humility isn't. Some people seem to have a nagging suspicion that humility really requires embracing something that is not real. They entertain the notion that someone needs to pretend that they are less gifted or talented than they really are in order to be humble. But this is not humility. Others think of humility as a kind of introspection that constantly scrutinizes all the inner thoughts and motives that produce their actions. Yet, this is also not humility. Still others equate humility with a personality trait that is nonassertive—a kind of passive quietism. Still, the essence of humility is bypassed.

True humility is the farthest notion from unreality—it is rooted and grounded in realism. The word *humility* is derived from the word from which we also get the word *humus.* It has to do with being "of the earth." *Humility,* in its essence, is the posture of spirit and frame of mind that freely acknowledges we are bound to earthly and lowly powers, unless a power from a higher order draws us up and incorporates us into itself—like a plant draws minerals from the dirt for its use.

This is similar to the way that God lifts us up in Christ and incorporates us into His kingdom. Humility embraces being in a place of dependency without shame. To honor God as our superior is not condemning; it is liberating, for it is reality and good news. It leads us to worship and serve Him out of awe, love and gratitude—things for which we are designed—and fills us with a sense of joy and well-being. A spirit of humility hopes and trusts for God and His kingdom mercifully to condescend, intervene, lay hold of and mold us into vessels that are made useful for higher and nobler purposes than we could ever attain left to our low estate. It delights to be clay in the hands of a master potter.

Humility knows that our greatest value is found in the treasure that God Himself has deposited in these "earthen vessels" through Christ. Humility affirms that, left to ourselves, we are poor in spirit, and it trusts for the riches of God's kingdom to come to us as a free gift and flow through us by God's mercy. Humility is not gained by looking down upon ourselves. Rather, it is apprehended by standing next to something that is immeasurably large and recognizing the contrast between that thing and us.

We as redeemed human beings should humble ourselves for four reasons: Because we are *creatures* of God, because we are *sinners* before God, because we are *servants* of God and because we are *children* of God. We don't have to lower ourselves to *be* these things—we already *are* these things! We have really great reasons to humble ourselves. This is why presenting our bodies to God as living sacrifices is our "spiritual service of worship" (Rom. 12:2, NAS). It is simply embracing reality to acknowledge our lower place before our God who is highly exalted. And although we bear the complications of being fallen beings, we also bear the dignity of being made and remade in Christ into the image of God.

Another highly motivating truth regarding humility is the fact that God Himself is humble. This is an amazing doctrine. It is most exemplified in the incarnation—God the Son taking on human form and laying His life down for us:

> Let this mind be in you which was also in Christ Jesus, who, being in the form of God, did not consider it robbery to be equal with God, but made Himself of no reputation, taking the form of a bond-servant, and coming in the likeness of men. And being found in appearance as a man, He humbled Himself and became obedient to the point of death, even the death of the cross. Therefore God also has highly exalted Him and given Him the name which is above every name, that at the name of Jesus every knee should bow, of those in heaven, and of those on earth, and of those under the earth, and that every tongue should confess that Jesus Christ is Lord, to the glory of God the Father.
>
> —PHILIPPIANS 2:5–11

Jesus let His own creation mock Him, spit on Him and put Him to death as a common criminal. If God can humble Himself, surely we can do the same without doing damage to our essential dignity. God's humility is also revealed in His choice to inhabit redeemed human beings by His Spirit. He has longed to make a way for Him to live inside of us. Through what Jesus has done, this has now become possible. I have often pondered the question that if I were God, would I choose to live inside of weak and sinful human beings? His humility is absolutely astounding.

> Or do you not know that your body is the temple of the Holy Spirit who is in you, whom you have from God, and you are not your own?
> —1 CORINTHIANS 6:19

True humility involves the ability to acknowledge to ourselves, and even to others, that we have done something well when we really have. It is said in Scripture that Moses was the meekest man on the face of the earth. But this was not mock humility—he apparently wrote it about himself! Humility simply implies that we would have been just as glad about something we've done well if someone else had done it! Humility doesn't deny beauty, strength, wisdom or talent wherever or in whomever such things manifest. But it does refuse to put others down or hold others down in an attempt to appear better than it really is. When someone expresses thanks for some service rendered, a humble person says, "You're welcome."

An acquaintance of mine tells the story of how at one time he gave a rather good sermon. After the service a new believer thanked him for his words that day. In mock humility he said, "Oh, that wasn't *me*. It was the *Lord*."

To this she replied, "Well it wasn't *that* good." He got "busted" by the Lord that day. Now he just says "thank you" to people when they compliment him!

Many years ago after I began to preach publicly and started to be complimented, I struggled to know how to respond to the Lord and other people over this dynamic. I knew that Jesus warned us not to "seek" or even "receive" the honor that comes from one another.

> How can you believe, who receive honor from one another, and do not seek the honor that comes from the only God?
>
> —JOHN 5:44

One day as I was talking to the heavenly Father about this, I saw a picture of a little trampoline superimposed over my heart. However, it was tipped upward like a satellite dish. I understood that the Lord was instructing me on how to deal with the praise of others. He was showing me that when the anointing of the Spirit through me touches people and they show their gratitude, then I should sincerely accept their thanks but then allow the glory to "rebound" off of my heart and be presented at the footstool of His throne. God wants us to give Him genuine credit for the ways in which He is pleased to use us.

True humility does not lead us to look down upon ourselves. It possesses a liberating self-unconsciousness. When Moses came down from the mountain after communing with God, he was unconscious of the fact that his face was radiating God's glory. The reaction of others had to inform him of this reality. There is a healthy self-examination in which we are to engage, but it is to be a "guided tour" of our interior life by the Holy Spirit who alone knows us as we need to be known. There is a counterfeit to this—a morbid and paralyzing introspection. Some people in their quest to be humble become quite proud of their attempt to be so. True humility knows the flowing rhythms of healthy spirituality—upward to God, inward to self and outward to others.

True humility is not the antithesis of spiritual boldness or confidence. Only the truly humble can be truly bold and filled with faith.

> Therefore, as it is written: "Let him who boasts boast in the Lord."
> —1 CORINTHIANS 1:31, NIV

These qualities are a work of the grace of God in a human soul. A humble person is dependent upon God, and in that condition, God imparts the kind of boldness and faith that He alone possesses into a person. Dependency is possibly the supreme quality of being childlike before God. This is a characteristic that we must never outgrow no matter how mature we become. The most spiritually mature are those who become the most dependent upon God.

Certainly another vital characteristic of childlikeness is a teachable spirit.

> Come to Me, all you who labor and are heavy laden, and I will give you rest. Take My yoke upon you and learn from Me, for I am gentle and lowly in heart, and you will find rest for your souls. For My yoke is easy and My burden is light.
> —MATTHEW 11:28–30

Maintaining the posture of being learners before God is the key to spiritual growth. A learner is able to admit failure without being wiped out by it. Rather, he learns from it, dusts off his embarrassment and tries again.

THE STAIRWAY OF HUMILITY

I had a prophetic vision once in which I saw a stairway. Strangely, I knew that somehow it only led *downward*. It led to a basement floor, which was solid and very clean. Then I saw words written on each of the six steps—conviction, contrition, confession, repentance, receiving and reaping. The first four are self-explanatory, but the last two beg some definition. I understood that "receiving" involved the "poverty of spirit" that we must come into to walk in God's kingdom. Jesus said that we are to freely receive and freely give (Matt. 10:8). The order here is immutable. We simply will not have the stuff to give to others unless we first receive it from God. Neither will we *freely* give it to others unless we are convinced that we didn't deserve or earn what God has given to us. It takes humility to be a good receiver.

The last step immediately reminded me of another vision I had seen many years before this. I saw a man before a large field with a sickle in his hand. He had been placed there by God to reap a negative harvest (difficult and complicated circumstances in his life) from what he had previously sown through years of unbelief and sin. As he stood there, he was complaining to God, even though he had recently become a believer. He was saying, "God, I thought You forgave me for all the sinful things that I had done. Why do I have to reap this harvest? This is going to be really hard. I don't know if I'll get through it."

Then I saw up in the sky these huge arms (God's) that were folded as if to imply that He was not going to move a muscle until this man finished reaping that whole field.

Next, I saw another man who was in the exact same situation. He had also recently become a believer. However, his attitude was completely different. He was saying, "God, thank You for forgiving me for all the horrible things that I have done. I know that I don't deserve this kind of freedom. I know that I'm going to have to reap this field, and I know it's going to be hard work. One thing is for sure—I'm not going to go back to living that way again. I really hate sin now, and reaping this field will remind me to fear Your name. Lord, I love You, and I praise You." Then he began to reap a corner of the field with a cheerfulness and gratitude in his heart.

Then, I saw those great arms in the sky again. Only this time, it was as though this man's praise rose up to God with such a force that He was moved with great compassion toward this man. Suddenly, God reached down with His right arm and grasped the whole field of grain with one hand. He easily plucked up the whole crop out of the ground and held it there for the man to see. Then He said, "Because you have learned to hate evil and to fear and love My name, you will not have to reap this field. This is My mercy toward you." With that, the vision ended.

I then understood what this last step in the stairway vision meant. We have to be willing before God to reap whatever He deems necessary from our living foolishly in the past. We must praise Him for His great kindness toward us in Christ and cast ourselves upon His mercy to deliver us as He sees fit from the complications that sin has produced in our circumstances of life.

I didn't even realize that this vision of the stairway

contained a word play until I shared it publicly for the first time. This stairway of humility led to "abasement." This quality of spirit is called *lowliness* in the Scripture, and the value of it has been lost in our culture and even in Christian circles. But Jesus and the apostles held lowliness forth as a good thing that opens the way for spiritual rest, peace and reconciliation between people. (See Matthew 11:25–30; Ephesians 4:1.) Besides, the lowly person has a great advantage—no one can put him down! He is thereby liberated to spend his spiritual, emotional, mental and physical energies in pursuits other than trying to avoid being somehow humiliated by others. He is caught up in seeking ultimately to please the only one Person whose approval really counts—God Himself. A humble person is willing to look bad if it is necessary for a greater good to be established. He also knows that he is not irreplaceable in the kingdom of God—God is able to raise up stones to praise Him if nothing else will glorify Him.

HUMILITY AND THE PROPHETIC

Now we turn to the question of how humility applies to prophetic ministry. First, it involves a number of the things to which I have already alluded—being accountable to the written Word of God and to spiritual leadership, being willing to confess mistakes and misses, packaging prophecies in ways that are respectful of the authorities of church leaders and individuals and so forth. But there are several problems that the presence of spiritual pride seems more specifically to create.

First, there is the illegal use of supernatural prophetic knowledge to undermine the credibility of others, to sow suspicion and division among friends, to gain leverage in interpersonal relationships, to extract loyalties and to engage in other similar kinds of manipulative behavior. This might be termed "knowledge brokering." This is the kind of thing that goes on in the world every day with people who are in situations and positions that make them privy to otherwise unknown information. However, this kind of thing has no place in the community of God's people.

> But we have renounced the hidden things of shame, not walking in craftiness nor handling the word of God deceitfully, but by manifestation of the truth commending ourselves to every man's conscience in the sight of God.
>
> —2 CORINTHIANS 4:2

Second, there is the problem of *elitism* that can creep in and grow up to characterize prophetic individuals and groups. Experiencing supernatural revelation can be "heady wine," and people have too often begun to think of themselves more highly than they ought to after having drunk it over a period of time. A subtle temptation comes at people who have been blessed with spiritual gifts. After they become used to their presence and operation, it is easy to take them for granted and even subconsciously start to entertain the idea that God originally gave them on the basis of merit. This allows a mentality of superiority to be set up within that person or group. Paul addressed this issue with the Corinthians:

> For who makes you different from anyone else? What do you have that you did not receive? And if you did receive it, why do you boast as though you did not?
>
> —1 CORINTHIANS 4:7, NIV

The apostle needed to remind these gifted believers about the basis of God's grace, which was the source of their spiritual abilities. The "pride of grace" and "religious pride" may be the most obnoxious forms of pride that exist. We must vigilantly guard against allowing such a place in our hearts.

Another application of humility in the prophetic has to do with the importance of listening. We mustn't forget that listening, not speaking, is the basis of the prophetic. It is first of all listening to God:

> The Sovereign LORD has given me an instructed tongue, to know the word that sustains the weary. He wakens me morning by morning, wakens my ear to listen like one being taught.
>
> —ISAIAH 50:4, NIV

The instructed tongue that is equipped to speak a word in its season to the weary is informed by the grace of God, which opens the ear of the teachable. But listening to God is just the first part. We must also seek to listen empathetically to people if we are going to be effective in the prophetic ministry. Too often people think that prophecy primarily has to do with speaking. I have found that listening and watching are more often the critical factors. The Scripture says that we should be "swift to hear, slow to speak" (James 1:19). This is good advice for anyone who wants to learn to prophesy. The art of listening has fallen on hard times in our day of self-absorption and impatience. We must learn to listen without having our "answer running." If we will discipline ourselves to listen better to people, we may in the process hear the very voice of God speaking to us.

BEING DISPLAYED AS WEAK

One of the most challenging lessons prophetic ministers need to learn is that the Lord sometimes will choose to present us before people as weak vessels. Not only will we be tested when the Lord calls us to speak a difficult word, but we will also be tested to the core of our being when people are expecting us to speak a word and the Lord is simply not giving us one to speak. Will we be able to be silent when the Spirit is not revealing anything?

This particular test came my way from the Lord last year when my friend Craig Smith, who is a pastor and musician from Arkansas, and I were ministering at David Ruis' Vineyard church in Winnipeg, Canada. We had had an effective weekend of ministry there. The Holy Spirit had provided a number of helpful prophetic words for people on the first day at a leaders' retreat. On the last night of our visit, a number of churches had come together to minister to the Lord with hopes and expectations that there would be time of significant prophetic ministry. After Craig had led us in a time of intimate and anointed worship, I came forward and gave a brief exhortation from the Scriptures. Then I offered myself to the Lord with hopes of being used in the prophetic. However, the Holy Spirit was not giving me any kind of inspiration or illumination for any of the five hundred or so people gathered that night. I encouraged them to wait upon the Lord with me a bit longer, which they graciously did. In fact, we waited quite a long time! All I could do was describe to them what "wasn't happening." They were a wonderful group of believers who had been fervently seeking the Lord. As far as I could tell, the Holy Spirit was not being quenched or grieved in any way. I believe that the Lord just wanted me to be displayed before them as weak. Maybe that *was* the prophetic message that God wanted to "speak" to them on that particular night. We decided to close the meeting early and encouraged people to go out and take time to fellowship with each other.

Many years ago, David Welday, who is one of the vice presidents of Strang Communications Company (the publisher of this book), was a part of the student fellowship that I was leading at Miami University in Ohio. Dave gave a wonderful illustration to our group that I have always remembered. In this illustration he compared a Christian to a glove and likened the Spirit of the Lord to a mighty hand that slips into the glove now and then. It's amazing what flimsy gloves can do when such a hand is within them. It can also be rather humiliating to discover what a glove cannot do when that hand has been withdrawn!

Of course, God doesn't actually withdraw from us. But many times the Lord will withdraw our awareness of His conscious presence and the supernatural anointing of the Holy Spirit for ministry. The anointing for the indwelling of the Spirit always abides within us. However, the anointing to move in miraculous power comes and goes at God's pleasure.

The Holy Spirit not only leads us into ministry, but there are times when he actually forbids us to do ministry.

> Now when they had gone through Phrygia and the region of Galatia, they were forbidden by the Holy Spirit to preach the word in Asia. After they had come to Mysia, they tried to go into Bithynia, but the Spirit did not permit them.
>
> —Acts 16:6–7

This dynamic teaches us not to be presumptuous before God. It also reinforces to our souls how dependent we truly are upon Him to engage in Spirit-led service. We must be filled with the Holy Spirit again and again as we minister in the gifts of the Spirit under the anointing of the Spirit. It's just the way God has designed it to work.

Handling Prophetic Mystique

There is an intrinsic "mystique" that accompanies prophecy. After all, it is the living God directly communicating His word to us humans. When people get around others who have a reputation for being prophetic, they usually experience heightened emotions—both hopes and fears. They wonder how much or how little God has told that prophetic person about them. They wonder if that person is hiding divine information from them. They are afraid that God has revealed to that person their worst weaknesses and sins. They wonder if God has told that person anything about their future. The interpersonal dynamics of this can get very weird for both parties!

Some prophetic-type people are quite in touch with this mystique, and sadly, they seek to take advantage of it in various ways. They use it to get "more" out of others— more affection, honor, money, commitments or loyalty. However, this is a far cry from the example of Jesus and the apostles. Jesus often took steps to hide the mystique that surrounded His ministry of power. Sometimes He told people to tell no one about their supernatural healing. At other times He left the crowd to be in solitude. He refused to allow people to make Him a political leader, because He knew it was His Father's will to lead Him to the cross.

I exhort prophetic people to "cloak" this intrinsic

mystique surrounding prophetic power and the influence that goes with it regularly and deliberately. The gifts of God and the word of God have their own power and can stand on their own. We should seek to hold out these things to people plainly and forthrightly as God anoints us and not add our "two bits" to help God out.

We need to understand that if we move in the supernatural gifts of God, there will be people (and demons) who will pressure us to work to become something that God hasn't ordained for us, either at this time or ever. This is why we should seek to be "naturally supernatural" in our style of relating and ministry. This is why it is vital for us to be transparent about our failures and weaknesses. We must seek to consciously and deliberately defuse the social power of this mystique rather than get any personal "strokes" from it. If we "cheat" in this matter, it will at some point turn around and "bite" us in one way or another. We need to deal squarely with our fleshly ambition and the lust for power over others.

When I was a young minister, there were times when I would struggle when some of the highly respected leaders from the movements with which I was identified would come to the area to minister in our churches. Sometimes I would be left out of the important strategic meetings, or no one would seem to care about my perspectives on the issues with which we were dealing. I think almost everyone knows what I am talking about here. Yet, as I look back on that season of my life, I am really thankful to the Lord for that testing of my heart and my ambitions.

One day I took a very long walk in the woods and talked my feelings out with the Lord. On that day I came to a deeper realization of something that I believe is vital for every believer to wrestle through. I came to terms with the truth that if God Himself, without my assistance, didn't raise me up into "higher levels" of authority, recognition and opportunity, then I *really didn't want* to "go there." (Incidentally, those realms of prominent ministry aren't all they are "cracked up to be" anyway!) I realized that otherwise I would be attempting to fill a role in the body of Christ that God would not be giving me the grace to fulfill. It seemed to me that this would expose me to unnecessary satanic attack, natural stress and a host of other distractions that I really didn't need or want.

I left something behind in the woods that day, which, by God's grace, I never picked up again in the way I had before: a striving, insecure, self-promoting and ambitious spirit. It was as if a thousand pounds had lifted off of my soul. Now when I am overlooked, ignored, bypassed, disregarded, written off, misunderstood, slandered, left out or picked last by mere humans, I seek to obtain that secret delight of knowing that my Lord is near me and His power is resting upon me in the "weakness" of my situation. Yes, it does still happen from time to time in my life—God sees to that!

Also on that day I did hear a clear word from the Spirit that was spoken to my heart. It was, "Michael, you focus on the depth of your ministry before Me, and I will take care of the breadth of your ministry before men." In connection to this I thought about the image of the cross and how the vertical beam is longer than the horizontal one.

Ask the Father in heaven to bring you to a place where you can sincerely acknowledge and confess as I did that fateful day: "Lord, I *really don't* want to be or do *more* than You have called me to be and do. I don't want to be or do *less* either. I just want to be and do what You have *truly ordained* for me to be and do in every season of my life."

173

This attitude can bring a contentment into our souls and guard us from wrongly utilizing the mystique that surrounds prophetic ministry instead of relying upon the Person and anointing of the Holy Spirit in our ministry.

Out of a deep insecurity, many people work hard to create the "right" emotional environment in trying to "get the Spirit moving." Actually, the Holy Spirit is a very secure Person, and He is very willing to move without human assistance:

> The wind blows wherever it pleases. You hear its sound, but you cannot tell where it comes from or where it is going.
>
> —JOHN 3:8, NIV

My paraphrase of John 3:8 is, "The Holy Spirit has a mind of His own." Our job is not to create "just the right environment" for Him to move, but normally it is simply to discern how He is already moving and try not to get left behind! Now I don't want to be misunderstood here. I am not suggesting that God does not use human mediation in the ministry of the Spirit's power and grace. Indeed, the Holy Spirit regularly makes Himself available to us with a degree of humility and vulnerability that astounds me. After all, He is God! Oftentimes, His divine promptings are so subtle that it seems as though He is almost placing the initiative in our laps. And it is important that we move boldly out in ministry trusting the Spirit to back us up.

My real point is that there is typically too much human energy and striving evident in circles of believers who value prophecy. Two pictures come to mind from the Scriptures when I think of this dynamic. The first is in

Luke 4 where Jesus reads about Himself being the anointed One of whom Isaiah spoke. There was no music, no drum roll, no microphones, lights or amps, no fanfare and not even any fans—He just said it and then sat down in that very ordinary first-century Jewish synagogue. Some people say they have to jump and scream when they get the anointing. Jesus sat down when He got anointed! Come to think of it, He sat down a second time after being crowned as both Lord and Christ—this time in heaven at the right hand of the Father after His resurrection and ascension! Maybe we too can sit down sometimes without quenching the Spirit.

The other picture I think of is Elijah at the spiritual showdown on Mt. Carmel. He was pretty cool in that situation. The four hundred false prophets of Baal did their thing to try to get the fire to fall on their sacrifice. After their grand failure, Elijah prepares the sacrifice and then asked for some water to be poured over the sacrifice. There are probably many reasons why he did this, but what stands out to me is that Elijah was confident in the power of God's heavenly fire not to be quenched by a little bit of Israeli water. He didn't have them put lighter fluid on it and then prepare to flick a match behind his back just in case God didn't "show up!"

RELIGIOUS "HYPE"

The final point I want to make on applying humility to prophecy has to do with the all too common problem of hyperbole (or hype) among people who claim to be prophetic. There simply has been too much showmanship, affected and learned religious behavior and too many slick methodologies employed among people who claim to be

Spirit-filled and Spirit-led believers. These kinds of things actually detract from the manifestation of the true power and glory of God. I believe that God is calling for a kind of prophetic people who will say in their hearts that they have had their fill of religious "hamburger helper" and who will not settle for anything but the "real meat" of the New Testament quality of prophetic gifting and ministry.

I heard an apparently true story about a group of believers who were accustomed to changing their language into "King James" English when they would prophesy. A small group of serious-minded "prophets" from the congregation came forward to prophesy over a newly converted young man. They laid their hands upon him, and then one man bellowed out with great authority, "Thus saith the Lord..." There was a moment of solemn silence as he dramatically paused and then sheepishly continued—"...I forgetest thy name." The poor fellow who was primed for a direct word from God suddenly discovered that God had apparently forgotten who he was!

We encourage people who prophesy first to try to relax and calm themselves, and not to change their language style in an attempt to make a greater impact—and then just deliver the message.

Sometimes people are genuinely caught up by the Spirit as they minister, and they are physically and emotionally affected by it. However, it is important to understand that this is not necessary for effective and anointed prophecy to happen. Too many people have gotten the idea that this kind of speech, behavior or phenomena is to accompany the "true" anointing of the Spirit. For some, this kind of thing has become "learned" religious behavior, and it actually discredits genuine supernatural ministry. I believe in ecstatic spiritual experiences, but when people seem always to be having them "on cue," then the credibility of their claim of inspiration actually goes down.

If ecstatic behavior happens to accompany the operation of spiritual gifts, then it is not wise to draw undue or extra attention to it as though it should automatically be viewed as a confirming sign of some kind. The impartation of the content of the gift itself is the important element, not the way in which the minister is being affected.

This style of prophetic ministry I am advocating may come off as less heroic, but it will be more helpful. When prophecy is brought forth, it is really much more for the sake of those to whom it is directed than it is for those who minister it. This is the spirit of servanthood that is to characterize all forms of ministry that's done in the name of Jesus. And if God is gracious to bless you and use you in the prophetic, try not to celebrate like the present-day American professional football players who "hot dog it" in the end zone when they score. Let us leave the "hype" in the arena of sports and games where it belongs—not in the arena of ministry done for the glory of Jesus Christ. Rather, take the advice of one of the college coaches who told his players, "If you get in the end zone, act like you've been there before." Then when you get alone before the Lord, let Him know how excited you are, and celebrate to your heart's content!

Chapter 9

What Does Passionate Pursuit Involve?

JESUS SAID THAT the greatest commandment was to love
God with every fiber of our being and then to love
our neighbor as ourselves. (See Mark 12:30–31.)
However, this commandment, like other standards of
living of which Jesus often spoke, is outside of our moral
reach if left to ourselves. The good news of Jesus Christ is
that we have not been left to ourselves—He has come to
us. He has come to forgive us of our sins and declare us
righteous through His substitutionary death and resurrection. He has come to us to actually dwell within us by His
Spirit. And He has done this out of His great love for us.

John said that this is the essence of love—not that we
loved God, but that He first loved us and gave His life for
us. God's love for us is the fountainhead of our responsive
love for Him and our fellow man. Knowing and believing
His passion for us is the basis of our passion for Him and
our compassion for others. This is a clear and undeniable

principle of the biblical teaching on God's kind of love—
"We love [God and others] because he first loved us" (1
John 4:19, NIV).

Spiritual hunger and thirst is often spoken of in Scripture
as a quality in which God takes great delight. God wants
us to seek after Him and the blessings that He has said He
wants to give us. God wants to be wanted, and He challenges us again and again to vigorously pursue after Him
and the things of His kingdom. Effort is not earning—this
kind of striving is not to be automatically categorized as or
confused with "legalism." Numerous passages within the
New Testament affirm this truth:

> And without faith it is impossible to please God,
> because anyone who comes to him must believe
> that he exists and that he rewards those who
> earnestly seek him.
>
> —HEBREWS 11:6, NIV

> Blessed are those who hunger and thirst for right
> eousness, for they will be filled.
>
> —MATTHEW 5:6, NIV

> Ask and it will be given to you; seek and you will find;
> knock and the door will be opened to you. For
> everyone who asks receives; he who seeks finds; and
> to him who knocks, the door will be opened. Which of
> you, if his son asks for bread, will give him a stone? Or
> if he asks for a fish, will give him a snake? If you, then,
> though you are evil, know how to give good gifts to
> your children, how much more will your Father in
> heaven give good gifts to those who ask him!
>
> —MATTHEW 7:7–11, NIV

> And from the days of John the Baptist until now the kingdom of heaven suffers violence, and the violent take it by force.
>
> —MATTHEW 11:12

As has been mentioned before, there is specific apostolic injunction to especially desire to prophesy. It is not wrong or selfish to desire to experience the prophetic power of the Holy Spirit.

> Follow the way of love and eagerly desire spiritual gifts, especially the gift of prophecy. For anyone who speaks in a tongue does not speak to men but to God. Indeed, no one understands him; he utters mysteries with his spirit. But everyone who prophesies speaks to men for their strengthening, encouragement and comfort. He who speaks in a tongue edifies himself, but he who prophesies edifies the church. I would like every one of you to speak in tongues, but I would rather have you prophesy. He who prophesies is greater than one who speaks in tongues, unless he interprets, so that the church may be edified.
>
> —1 CORINTHIANS 14:1–5, NIV

The context of 1 Corinthians 14 seems to indicate that there is a kind of prophecy in the church in which any believer can potentially operate. There have been moments in my experience when the presence of the Holy Spirit in a gathering of believers has been such that it could be said that a "spirit of prophecy" was resting upon the congregation. In this environment, I have seen people, who never before had consciously experienced discerning the voice of God, quickly and effortlessly receive impressions, pictures and words from the Holy Spirit. Of course, it is actually impossible to become a Christian without "hearing the voice of God." And in this most fundamental sense, all true believers have tasted of the prophetic spirit:

> No one can come to me unless the Father who sent me draws him, and I will raise him up at the last day. It is written in the Prophets: "They will all be taught by God." Everyone who listens to the Father and learns from him comes to me.
>
> —JOHN 6:44–45, NIV

MY CONVERSION STORY

My conversion to Jesus Christ at age eighteen is directly traceable to hearing the "voice" of God. After my supernatural conviction at age sixteen that I recounted in the second chapter of this book, I sought to run away from the truth that God had told to me. Just days after I graduated from Eisenhower High School just north of Utica, Michigan, the Lord graciously began to engage me by the Holy Spirit. I had taken a job as an appliance and furniture delivery man for a local furniture store. For a period of a week and a half in June of 1973, the Spirit began to speak to me in what I now understand to be the "internal audible voice." I can still remember with clarity some of the exact phrases that He said to me: "I want you to follow Me." "I want you to be My servant." "I want you to surrender every major decision in your life to Me—where you go to school, what kind of career you will have, where you will live, whom you will marry—I want everything."

I had never heard of such things before. I remembered

hearing both from my older brother and from the church I had attended one time that Jesus Christ was the way to the Father. I knew that this was about becoming a Christian, but I had no conception of the grace of God. I knew the power of sinful desires and that these were alive in my soul. In fact, I felt very guilty about this. I imagined that becoming a Christian would involve me choosing to believe in and follow Jesus, forcing myself to "go straight" and gritting my teeth in preparation to live a boring and miserable life as a Christian. Yet, I was miserable as I was, and I knew that if I became a Christian, I would go to heaven when I died.

For that week and a half, I literally could not get those thoughts out of my head day or night. My resistance was breaking down, and one sunny day I made my decision to become a Christian. I parked the truck behind the store, got out of the cab, looked up into the sky and prayed my first prayer from my heart. Since I had no formal biblical training, I had no knowledge of the right language to use with which to "talk properly" to God.

I simply prayed, "You've got me; I give up." But I really meant it. Immediately, I had a vision (like a powerful daydream that suddenly invades the part of your brain that can see pictures) of myself standing on the very spot upon which I was literally standing. However, in the vision, my arms were raised up to heaven. At this point in my life I had never seen Christians raise their hands in worship. Then it was like a movie camera backing up, and I could see behind me. There was a huge hand holding a gun that was pointed into my back. I intuitively knew that it was the hand of God and that He was "arresting" me. I had been running away from Him for two years, and now He had caught up with me—and He was "busting" me for being a renegade. Then I understood why I had prayed—"You've got me; I give up." This helped me understand more clearly why Christians are called to raise their hands when they worship God. It's all about *unconditional surrender!*

I then had a second vision stranger than the first one. I saw a giant slab of rock that was about two feet thick and seven feet tall sitting squarely on top of my shoulders. It would have weighed tons, and it had notches cut out from the bottom of it to fit securely over my shoulders and head. I must have been carrying this thing around with me for some time, although it would have been humanly impossible to do so in the natural. Again, I instantly understood that this great slab represented the guilt of my sins and the guilt feelings that attended them. Next, I saw a bolt of lightning come out of the sky and strike the rock slab at its top with such force that the slab cracked through its width. The crack quickly descended down to the very bottom, at which time it fell off of me in two pieces. When the two pieces hit the ground, they made a terrific thud.

I felt as though I were going to float off into the air. I was so light after this great burden had been broken off of me. Then I heard that same internal audible voice say to me, "Your sins are totally and forever forgiven." Next, I had a distinct feeling that somehow Jesus Christ was actually coming into my soul. I had thought that the idea of "Jesus coming into your heart" was metaphorical. Now it was literally happening to me.

Then the most surprising thing happened. I realized that God was going to give me a greater passion to live in obedience to Him than I had ever had to live in sin. He was actually going to transform my inner desires and give me a power to walk them out—a power I could have never suspected would ever dwell within me. At once I realized that being a Christian was not going to be boring—this had been my greatest fear. Rather, I understood that it would be the greatest adventure upon which a human being could ever embark.

I immediately told my coworker Pat that I had just become a Christian. I was so shocked when he dropped his head and confessed that he also was a Christian, but that he wasn't walking with God. He said, "I think I need to get back with the Lord."

I replied with great assurance, for someone just a few minutes old in Christ, "That sounds right to me."

I was riding on the proverbial "cloud nine" for the next days as I would constantly marvel at the miracle that had happened in my life. I was so excited that God had forgiven me of my sins. I didn't have any biblical words to thank the Lord Jesus, so I would walk around my home saying things like, "Wow!" "Thank You!" "Oh, man!" "You made me a Christian!" "This is great!"

About one week after my conversion, I was walking around my home and had turned the corner from the kitchen into the dining room. A supernatural wind came across the room and hit me in the chest. But it didn't stop as it went right into my chest cavity and began to circulate within me like a cylinder of air on its side. I heard that same internal audible voice saying, "Don't be afraid; I'm doing something to you." So I stood there and just let it happen. Then suddenly I started to speak out in a language that I had never learned before. It was gushing out of me like a torrent of water. After it subsided, I remember saying, "God, before this I knew that You were real. Now I know that You are really, really real!"

At this time, my father, who had come to faith in

Jesus two years previously, gave me a little red New Testament that had some outlines in the front of it that led people through the basics of Christian faith. It had Scripture references with these notes. I started to devour reading this little Bible hour after hour. All of these passages began to make total sense to me, and I realized just how relevant the Bible is to all people of every generation.

As I continued to grow in my knowledge of God and His Holy Spirit, I began to understand the operation of the prophetic—and its function in the church today.

THE PROPHETIC SPECTRUM

The context of 1 Corinthians 12 and Romans 12, which are two other New Testament passages that describe spiritual gifts, seem to indicate that there is a kind of prophecy in the church in which not every believer will necessarily function. This might be described as someone who has been given by God a prophetic function, role, ministry or gift for the benefit of the body of Christ. Ephesians 4 describes people identified as "prophets" as being gifts to the church:

> It was he who gave some to be apostles, *some to be prophets,* some to be evangelists, and some to be pastors and teachers, to prepare God's people for works of service, so that the body of Christ may be built up until we all reach unity in the faith and in the knowledge of the Son of God and become mature, attaining to the whole measure of the fullness of Christ.
>
> —EPHESIANS 4:11–13, NIV, EMPHASIS ADDED

It is clear in this passage that not every Christian is called by God to be such. Here, as in 1 Corinthians 14, it seems it was normative in the first-century church to identify some members of the body as "prophets." The climax of the prophetic will apparently occur in the time just before the Second Coming of Christ when God raises up the "two witnesses" to be His special representatives in that hour of earth's history:

> And I will give power to my two witnesses, and they will prophesy for 1,260 days, clothed in sackcloth. These are the two olive trees and the two lamp-stands that stand before the Lord of the earth. [This is a clear reference to the prophecy in Zechariah 4.] If anyone tries to harm them, fire comes from their mouths and devours their enemies. This is how anyone who wants to harm them must die. These men have power to shut up the sky so that it will not rain during the time they are prophesying; and they have power to turn the waters into blood and to strike the earth with every kind of plague as often as they want.
>
> —REVELATION 11:3–6, NIV

Upon examining and comparing these Scriptures, I posit the concept that prophecy in the New Testament is on a "graduated spectrum," which includes:

- Hearing God unto personal conversion (which all Christians have experienced)

- Moving in simple inspirational prophecy (which can and should be sought after by all believers)

- The role of prophetic ministry (which typically involves more "weighty" revelation, is available to fewer, but might possibly be given by God if sought for)

- The ministry of a prophet (which is given only by the sovereign choice of God)

- The two witnesses of Revelation (who have already been selected by God from long ago)

Therefore, the lower half of the prophetic spectrum is more or less "there for the asking," while the upper half involves a specific divine calling upon a progressively narrowing field of individuals. With this model of prophetic experience, the various emphases and possible tensions of these abovementioned Scriptures, as well as others, are explained and synthesized.

God has apportioned to us by His will and choice for us a particular sphere of gifting and ministry. However, it does not imply that the principle of pursuing Him diligently for an enhancement of His anointing upon our gift is negated. Doing this is a part of good and wise stewardship on our part. Anyway, no one really knows if God might call us into and impart to us a measure of gifting greater than before. We only discover this as we abandon ourselves to cooperating with the Lord on our spiritual journey.

We also know from the ancient prophecy of Joel, which Peter quoted on the day of Pentecost (through which there was a partial fulfillment of the prophecy), that in the days just before the Second Coming of Christ there will be a worldwide outpouring of the Holy Spirit, which will be characterized primarily by the prophetic.

No, this is what was spoken by the prophet Joel: "In the last days, God says, I will pour out my Spirit on all people. Your sons and daughters will prophesy, your young men will see visions, your old men will dream dreams. Even on my servants, both men and women, I will pour out my Spirit in those days, and they will prophesy. I will show wonders in the heaven above and signs on the earth below, blood and fire and billows of smoke. The sun will be turned to darkness and the moon to blood before the coming of the great and glorious day of the Lord. And everyone who calls on the name of the Lord will be saved."

—ACTS 2:16–21, NIV

The implications of this prophecy are that the gift of prophecy has not ceased, that men, women, the old and the young can prophetically minister and that there will be an inevitable increase of prophetic experience as the Second Coming of Christ approaches. We had better get good at stewarding the prophetic gift, for there is only more to come!

I want to conclude this chapter with some very practical points that will round out the theme regarding how we might go about passionately pursuing prophecy in a way that keeps us within safe boundaries. All the risks will never be eliminated. They aren't supposed to be! However, some of them can be appropriately minimized if we will step back and look at the subject a little more objectively. May God raise up many loving and wise prophetic servants in the days ahead, and may they do exploits in His name.

TEN PRACTICAL SUGGESTIONS FOR
PURSUING THE PROPHETIC

1. Regularly expose yourself to solid basic training in the Scriptures.

2. Stay focused on doing the basics of Christian discipleship—worship, study, prayer, witnessing, fellowship and serving in the local church.

3. Deliberately engage in the classic spiritual disciplines—make time for personal meditation, prayer, worship, reflection, journaling, solitude and fasting from media. These things do not merit spiritual gifts, but can greatly enhance our sensitivity to the Holy Spirit.

4. Stir up the gift of prophecy by taking the risks involved in sharing words and impressions in the proper settings.

5. Muster the courage to risk again if you fail to any degree or even if you succeed. It is impossible to "rest on our laurels" with the prophetic. The testimony of yesterday's "hit" is not good enough for today or tomorrow.

6. Place yourself in spiritual environments in which believers are worshiping and waiting upon the moving of the Holy Spirit through the spiritual gifts. Experiences will inevitably come if you do so.

7. Listen to spiritual music to receive prophetic

inspiration. This happened with prophetic
people in Scripture.

8. Keep a record or journal of dreams, impres-
    sions, visions and so forth. Having these things
    recorded will help reveal patterns of communi-
    cation and symbolic language that God is using
    to speak to us. (I have found that keeping a
    microcassette by my bed has helped me to cap-
    ture and record many prophetic dreams that I
    would have otherwise forgotten.)

9. Expose yourself to scriptural teaching that spe-
    cifically addresses issues related to prophecy.

10. Hang around prophetic people if you can—
    there is an "osmosis principle" that operates with
    the prophetic gifting. Prophetic anointing can be
    "caught" and "imparted" from one person to
    another—this is one of the ways of God.

FIVE PRACTICAL OUTLETS FOR
DEVELOPING PROPHETIC MINISTRY

1. *Corporate prayer meetings*—Pray your revela-
    tion back to God and report your revelation to
    other intercessors when appropriate.

2. *Prayer line ministry*—Pray your impressions
    and prophesy over others who respond to invi-
    tations for personal ministry.

3. *Small groups and "one on one"*—This is prob-
    ably the best place to learn and grow in

prophecy. Ask for feedback from those around you who know you best concerning the degree of blessing your words have been to them.

4. *Sharing dreams and visions with church leaders and individuals*—Share with the leadership in written form the ones that seem the most applicable to the church.

5. *Prophesying in public services*—Following are some practical guidelines and suggestions regarding public prophecy.

- Trust God's providence working through worship leaders, pastoral leaders and other prophetic people—even if they may miss providing you an opportunity. God is bigger than these kinds of errors. He moves in seasons within the life of the church. Next week or month will probably end up being just as good as the present time for you to share your word.

- Discern the purpose of any given meeting and the mood and timing within the particular meeting. Come spiritually prepared and "prayed up" rather than relying on the music to help get you into spiritual sync.

> But in the church I would rather speak five intelligible words to instruct others than ten thousand words in a tongue. Brothers, stop thinking like children. In regard to evil be infants, but in your thinking be adults.
> —1 Corinthians 14:19–20, NIV

191

In this passage, Paul is challenging the believers to be mature in their stewarding of spiritual utterances. Think about the crowd to whom you're ministering, and serve them by "packaging" your words in ways that makes it easier for the people to hear, understand and appreciate your words.

- Wait for the right timing to speak. Often there comes a sense of the manifest presence of God when it is time to prophesy. Seek to flow with the current of the Spirit's broader movement and mood in the gathering. Double-check before speaking forth something that will redirect the course of the meeting.

- Spiritual leaders may ask you to share with them the gist of what you have received before sharing it with the congregation to help provide a confirmation to the content and timing of the prophecy. This is not too much to ask of members of the body in my thinking.

- Be straightforward and use plain language—"I believe the Lord is saying..." is better than "Thus saith the Lord..." I encourage people to try to avoid highly symbolic language and/or melodramatic language—it can be very difficult for people to follow.

- Be as concise as you can. Quickly get to and give the essence of the revelation.

- Utilize the Scripture when you prophesy. This can be very effective and a good place to begin.

Store it up in your heart and mind so the Spirit can easily draw upon it.

- Avoid unnecessary repetition—especially with songs.

- Don't sing your prophecy if you don't sing well. Ask a friend!

- Realize that authority and liberty in prophetic ministry grow naturally as you become proven through a good track record—don't demand titles and microphones. Wait upon God to raise you up and back you up.

Chapter 10

CATCHING THE FORERUNNER SPIRIT

THEOLOGICALLY SPEAKING, SALVATION and judgment are two sides of the same coin. This theme is regularly seen in the Book of Isaiah, as well as in several other Old Testament books of the prophets. Salvation is the application of God's *righteousness* or *justice* in relation to humanity. God doesn't save us simply because He is *nice*. He has been gracious to save us because He has *dealt justly* with the problem of sin through the finished work of Jesus Christ our Lord. When God moves in the earth, it always involves both salvation and judgment—the humble are saved and the proud of heart are judged through the same move of the Holy Spirit. Sometimes, the nature and reality of this judgment is hidden from human eyes. However, in time it will be manifested, if it is not immediately measured out.

There is a concept that is a vital to a general understanding of the prophetic ministry. God is—and has always been—committed to working through human prophetic voices to *prepare* both His people and the nations as a whole for His divine activity—whether it be salvation or judgment. God lets His friends the prophets hear about His secret plans in advance so that they might intercede, warn and proclaim in order hopefully to minimize human disobedience and its negative fallout upon the earth.

> Surely the Lord GOD does nothing, unless He reveals His secret to His servants the prophets.
>
> —AMOS 3:7

GOD'S FORERUNNERS

This ministry of prophetic preparation is sometimes referred to as a "forerunner ministry." Prophetic "heralds" are sent ahead of the Lord to announce the coming visitation of the King to the people. This was literally the method of communication employed in ancient cultures when kings were intending to pay a visit somewhere. This was also the way that new laws and proclamations were communicated throughout a kingdom. (See 2 Chronicles 30.)

> So they resolved to make a proclamation throughout all Israel, from Beersheba to Dan, that they should come to keep the Passover to the LORD God of Israel at Jerusalem, since they had not done it for a long time in the prescribed manner. Then *the runners* went throughout all Israel and Judah with the letters from the king and his leaders, and spoke according to the command of the king: "Children of Israel,

> return to the LORD God of Abraham, Isaac, and Israel;
> then He will return to the remnant of you who have
> escaped from the hand of the kings of Assyria."
> —2 CHRONICLES 30:5–6, EMPHASIS ADDED

Jesus Christ Himself is the prototypical forerunner who, in this case, has *gone before* His redeemed people into heaven itself to prepare the way for our future arrival.

> This hope we have as an anchor of the soul, both
> sure and steadfast, and which enters the Presence
> behind the veil, where *the forerunner* has entered
> for us, even Jesus, having become High Priest for-
> ever according to the order of Melchizedek.
> —HEBREWS 6:19–20, EMPHASIS ADDED

Another prominent and prototypical "forerunner" in the Scriptures is Elijah. (Moses certainly was as well.) Elijah was empowered at times literally to "run" by the power of God—a historical fact that also holds symbolic meaning as a "word picture."

> Then the hand of the LORD came upon Elijah; and he
> girded up his loins and ran ahead of Ahab to the
> entrance of Jezreel.
> —1 KINGS 18:46

Elijah stood before the Lord in the Spirit, received God's counsel and boldly delivered his message to the whole nation of Israel and its leaders. The Lord backed up his prophetic prayer with signs in the heavens and wonders upon the earth.

> And Elijah the Tishbite, of the inhabitants of Gilead,

said to Ahab, "As the LORD God of Israel lives, before
whom I stand, there shall not be dew nor rain these
years, except at my word."

—1 KINGS 17:1

Elijah was raised up by God to proclaim God's dis-
ciplinary judgment upon the compromising nation of
Israel. He was also used as a prophetic human catalyst
for national repentance and revival though a power
encounter with the prophets of Baal on Mt. Carmel.

Many years after Elijah was translated to heaven,
Malachi was inspired by the Holy Spirit to utilize Elijah's
name and ministry in the context of preparing the way
for the coming of the Messiah to earth.

Behold, I will send you *Elijah the prophet* before the
coming of the great and dreadful day of the Lord.
And he will turn the hearts of the fathers to the children, and the hearts of the children to their fathers,
lest I come and strike the earth with a curse.

—MALACHI 4:5–6, EMPHASIS ADDED

By this imagery, the Holy Spirit was indicating that the
same kind of "prophetic forerunner" dynamics as seen in
Elijah's day would immediately precede the greatest
divine visitation of God—the "day of the Lord." (There
are many, many Scriptures into which this "day of the
Lord" language is tied.)

In the Old Testament, there were only hints regarding
the fact that the Messiah would come two times—first as
the "suffering Servant," and second as a "conquering
King." Most of the Jews expected Him only to come in
the second capacity. Some prophecies, as the one below,

referred to both of His comings in the "same breath," with no conceivable indication that over two thousand years would separate them. It was only as Israel's history unfolded throughout the centuries that it could be commonly understood exactly how they have been fulfilled. I imagine that some of the prophecies regarding the Second Coming will hold similar surprise applications for us all. Sometimes prophetic *hindsight* is as helpful and powerful as prophetic *foresight*.

> The Spirit of the Lord GOD is upon Me, because the LORD has anointed Me to preach good tidings to the poor; He has sent Me to heal the brokenhearted, to proclaim liberty to the captives, and the opening of the prison to those who are bound; To proclaim *the acceptable year of the LORD,* and the *day of vengeance of our God;* to comfort all who mourn…
> —ISAIAH 61:1–2, EMPHASIS ADDED

UNDERSTANDING THE KINGDOM

Just as a year is much longer than a day, the season of grace and mercy that has come to the earth through the good news of Jesus will linger over the nations much longer than the brief season of God's temporal judgments at the very end of this age. But that season of judgment will indeed come. Both of these elements, salvation and judgment, can be considered as part of the prophetic package included in the "day of the Lord." Moreover, before the final and ultimate fulfillment of the meaning of the "day of the Lord," there have been and will be "days of the Lord" that lead up to it. These seasons of refreshing, revival and divine judgment throughout the nations are historical tokens of the reality of the ultimate "day of the Lord." They are intended to stimulate faith and obedience toward God among humankind.

These moves of God are "windows" in human history though which "eschatological (future age) power" blows. New Testament theology is based in "kingdom theology." And kingdom theology is always bathed in the mystery and paradox of the tension between *this age* and *the age to come*. The kingdom of God is *really here,* but it is not *fully here*. If we do not embrace this theological tension, then we will be confused about many of God's truths and ways.

In light of this biblical framework for understanding the kingdom of God, it is very reasonable that the Messiah would come twice—first as a Savior and then again as a King and Judge. And, it follows that the "Elijah" of Malachi's prophecy would necessarily have *two appearings*. The first time he would herald the nearness of the first coming of Messiah. The final time, he would herald the nearness of His Second Coming. Jesus clearly alludes to this mystery.

> And His disciples asked Him, saying, "Why then do the scribes say that Elijah must come first?" Jesus answered and said to them, "Indeed, *Elijah is coming* first and will restore all things. But I say to you that *Elijah has come already,* and they did not know him but did to him whatever they wished. Likewise the Son of Man is also about to suffer at their hands." Then the disciples understood that He spoke to them of John the Baptist.
> —MATTHEW 17:10–13, EMPHASIS ADDED

Jesus speaks of the preparatory prophetic ministry of

the "Elijah" principle. He declares that he "is coming first" and that he "has already come." He also reveals that carnal people around at the time will not necessarily recognize "what on earth is going on." Of course, John the Baptist was the *initial fulfillment* of Malachi's word as the angel Gabriel announced to his father Zacharias:

> He will also go before Him in the spirit and power of Elijah, "to turn the hearts of the fathers to the children," and the disobedient to the wisdom of the just, to make ready a people prepared for the Lord.
> —LUKE 1:17

Surely, if there was a "forerunner ministry" that served to prepare the way for the first coming of Christ, there will be a similar ministry raised up by God "in the spirit and power of Elijah" to prepare both the church and the earth for the Second Coming—the culmination of God's purposes in human history. This is no mere theological "stretch"—it is simple, straightforward and clear.

A LAST-DAY VICTORIOUS CHURCH

The only other New Testament passage that refers to a "restoration of all things" is in the Book of Acts.

> Repent therefore and be converted, that your sins may be blotted out, so that times of refreshing may come from the presence of the Lord, and that He may send Jesus Christ, who was preached to you before, *whom heaven must receive until the times of restoration of all things, which God has spoken by*

*the mouth of all His holy prophets since the world
began.*
                                  —ACTS 3:19–21, EMPHASIS ADDED

I don't presume to understand all that "the restoration
of all things" implies, but I do believe that it is an important period of divine activity upon the earth during this
world's final generation that is linked to the "Elijah" forerunner ministry that comes on the scene and culminates
with the Second Coming of Christ. It sure sounds awesome, whatever it means exactly! It will be both "great"
and "terrible." Peter, in this passage in Acts, seemed to
anticipate "times of refreshing" (periodic reformations
and revivals) to come upon the church while the return
of Christ from heaven is delayed (now going on two
thousand years). He also implies that the generation in
which the "restoration of all things" takes place is a major
prophetic theme of the Scriptures.

It is this biblical paradigm that, more than anything,
establishes a proper prophetic expectation for a final
great global revival and a massive evangelistic harvest.
The Old Testament passage from which this interpretation of the church's future is drawn is Psalm 110. It is
referred to, directly and indirectly, in the New
Testament more than twenty times. This is four or five
times more often than any other Old Testament passage! We do well to pay attention to how the apostles
understood and used this passage to proclaim the
kingdom of Christ:

> The LORD said to my Lord,
> "Sit at My right hand,
> Till I make Your enemies Your footstool."

The LORD shall send the rod of Your strength out of
    Zion.
Rule in the midst of Your enemies!
Your people shall be volunteers
In the day of Your power;
In the beauties of holiness, from the womb of the
    morning,
You have the dew of Your youth.
The LORD has sworn
And will not relent,
"You are a priest forever
According to the order of Melchizedek."
The Lord is at Your right hand;
He shall execute kings in the day of His wrath.
He shall judge among the nations,
He shall fill the places with dead bodies,
He shall execute the heads of many countries.
He shall drink of the brook by the wayside;
Therefore He shall lift up the head.

—PSALM 110:1–7

Wherever we see the usage of the "right hand" language in the New Testament, it is a reference to an
understanding that Christ is *not waiting* to be crowned
King, but that He *already* has been crowned King of all
the kings of the earth—even though most of the earthly
kings haven't yet figured out who is in charge! He is
ruling now *in the midst* of His enemies. Jesus is reigning
now and waiting at the Father's right hand until His enemies are significantly subdued.

But this Man, after He had offered one sacrifice for
sins forever, sat down at the right hand of God,

from that time *waiting* till His enemies are made His footstool.

—HEBREWS 10:12–13, EMPHASIS ADDED

For what is Jesus waiting? He is actually waiting for His bride, the church, to rise up in the fullness of Christ, her Bridegroom, to volunteer freely to serve Him out of love and gratitude and to accomplish her ordained mission in the nations.

And Jesus came and spoke to them, saying, "All authority has been given to Me in heaven and on earth. Go therefore and make disciples of all the nations, baptizing them in the name of the Father and of the Son and of the Holy Spirit, teaching them to observe all things that I have commanded you; and lo, I am with you always, even to the end of the age." Amen.

—MATTHEW 28:18–20

Through His work on the cross and His subsequent resurrection and ascension, Christ stripped the kingdom of darkness of its legal hold over humanity. *However, He has allowed His enemies to remain active* because He desires for His Spirit-filled human partners to rise up and prevail over evil in the strength of the victory that He purchased for us with His own blood. This is a part of dignified privilege that Jesus wants to share with us as His coheirs and colaborers in His Father's kingdom. It is also a part of our training for ruling with Him in the ages to come.

Just as Jesus overcame the world, the flesh and the devil two thousand years ago, so now He wants the church also to overcome. In this age, the Spirit-filled church is the *primary agent* of God's kingdom on earth. We are called to "execute on them the written judgment" by effectively witnessing to all the nations regarding the good news of Jesus Christ, whether it results in conversions and discipleship or persecution and martyrdom. (See Psalm 149:9.) The End-Time church will have her portion in both. Whether by life or by death, Christians are called to subdue the rebellious rage of the ungodly spirits and people across the nations by patiently overcoming evil with good.

The victorious last-day church is not glib "triumphalism," "idealism," "reconstructionism," "escapism," "revivalism," "perfectionism" or "nationalism." The church's corporate strength and power is not in military, economic or political might—carnal "weapons." Her authority is spiritual and moral as she functions like a conscience among the nations. Her presence in the earth provides moral "salt and light"—preserving influence and truth—holding back both the full rage of Satan and the just wrath of God. The church is to stand in the spirit and mind-set of the great heroes of faith spoken of in Hebrews 11. They lived and died in faith as they submitted to the providence and purposes of God in their day. They set their eyes and hearts on the eternal city of God and lived as pilgrims and strangers in this age. They lived in the light of God's coming judgment and their everlasting reward.

These saints of God understood that their physical death was not the biggest event possible in human experience, but that coming to a living faith in God is. They crossed over the *big gap* in human life *before* their deaths. To pass through physical death into heavenly life is actually just a little step—a breath away. Without trying

204

to be insensitive or crude, let me say that, theologically speaking, our coming physical death as Christians (if the Lord tarries) is *not that big of a deal*. For us, this life is as bad as it gets. However, for unbelievers, this life is as good as it gets! This reality should move us to holy action.

God is beginning to pour out this "forerunner spirit" upon believers in our generation. The signs of an unprecedented global divine visitation are all around us.

- A global prayer movement
- A global worship movement
- A global evangelistic movement
- A global signs-and-wonders movement
- A global church growth movement
- A global interchurch, interorganizational networking effort
- A global expectation of revival

The "spirit and power of Elijah" is being made available to Christians like never before in the history of the church. This is truly exciting; however, I believe that this also implies that our greatest challenges lie ahead of us. The church is not going to just breeze through into uninterrupted victory—especially given her current condition!

Chapter 11

DEALING WELL
WITH JEZEBEL

I RECENTLY HAD AN unusual experience. I was preparing a sermon to preach in our fellowship from the Book of Ephesians called "Believe Right, Live Right, Fight Right." As I was sitting in my chair with my laptop computer on my lap, I started to receive clear thoughts that almost seemed as if I were "eavesdropping" on a vile conversation between a false teacher and an immature Christian. This is what I wrote as I "listened":

> Your efforts to become more holy are futile because they automatically lead to self-righteousness, legalism, a religious spirit and judgmentalism. The Holy Spirit is so powerful—you don't think He really needs your help, do you? Besides, you fall so far short of Christ's perfection that any progress is insignificant in comparison—so why try?
>
> We will all be made instantly perfect at the

Second Coming, so what's all the concern about holiness anyway? Our sinfulness actually magnifies the grace of God. I admit, I'm not perfect—but who is? Sure, sinning isn't good, but neither is it really that big of a deal in the end. Anyway, Jesus will just have to forgive me, even if I do sin. The major issue is that nobody has the right to judge me or confront me—even if I do have some weaknesses and a few struggles. Anyone who does is really the biggest sinner of all. Jesus said so. Just keep your spirit free and ward off that condemnation.

My God is into love, not discipline. Outward behaviors aren't that important because God only looks on the heart attitude, and no one knows my heart. Christianity is all about liberty—right? I can curse or swear when I'm upset because it's "real." God doesn't expect us to hide our "real" feelings, does He? Give me a break! It's not even emotionally healthy to try. Who's to say what a swear word is anyway?

I can handle a little bit of harmless flirting. Hey, my spouse isn't meeting my needs very well right now, and God made me to need companionship with the opposite sex. He's the one who has given me my nice body and good looks. I think He's actually proud of me when I show them off a little. If people pay more attention to me, then maybe I can win them for the Lord.

I have no problem with sexually explicit movies, either—I just watch them for their plots. Some of them have great special effects, too. Besides, Jesus said that it's not what goes into a person that defiles them, but what comes out.

207

The Spirit has given me liberty to drink alcohol, too. A few drinks help get my blood flowing, but don't make me drunk to where I'm out of control or anything. OK, I do get a little tipsy, but nobody can tell that anything is different, and I can still feel the Lord's presence all around me. Actually, drinking helps my circle of friends to have great times of fellowship. We have really busted that religious spirit.

And if I have to lie sometimes—especially to avoid staying out of the line of fire of these self-righteous do-gooders, then I will. I don't have to confess my sins to anyone but God. If they only knew what I have been through in my life, they wouldn't be so quick to judge me.

They just need to dial down for goodness' sake. The biggest problem in the church is people who are so proud about how they're "pressing into God" and "taking the kingdom by force"—what arrogance! They think all their fasting and prayer is really going to make a difference. Don't listen to them. We will outlast them if we can quietly spread this teaching about true liberty. They won't be able to keep up their intensity forever. God Himself will overthrow their pharisaical ideas. They aren't into the grace of God, but want to bring everybody under their legalistic rules.

Here's the best way I have found to handle them. Tell them how wonderful they are and how full of God's love and mercy they are, and they will get the message that they had better leave you alone. If this little bit of flattery doesn't work, then just rip into them with indignation for their self-righteousness. This will usually keep them off balance long enough for you to avoid a counter-confrontation, and it will give you

some time to rally some friends to stand with you if
they decide to approach you at a later time.

After I finished writing these words, I felt that I had
been having a prophetic encounter with the Spirit of God.
This "dialogue," filled with both half-truths and total lies,
is the kind of spiritually seductive force that gets into the
heads of many sincere but weak (or even just tired)
believers and undermines their confidence in standing for
righteousness and biblical ethics. I believe that many such
false teachers are lurking around Christian fellowships and
secretly spreading their versions of "Christian liberty."

Often, these are people who at one time were walking in
genuine fellowship with God, but they have gradually
backslidden in their hearts even though they have
remained *socially involved* with believers. They are under
pressure to create a "theology" to justify the expression of
the sinful passions and compromises to which they are progressively giving themselves. It isn't "politically correct" or
"socially convenient" for them just to face reality and admit
that the flow of genuine spiritual passion has dried up
within them, so they put a "spin" on the truth and attempt
to keep up the *image* of being a dedicated believer.

If they can succeed in persuading other Christians to
join them in this different and erroneous way of thinking
and living, then it bolsters their self-deception and, in
their eyes, lends credibility to their claim of everything
being OK in their relationship with God. Through the
years, I have watched this dynamic repeat itself in many
situations. A kind of *pseudospiritual sophistication* disguises itself as, and displaces, *spiritual maturity.*

And to the angel of the church in Thyatira write,

"These things says the Son of God, who has eyes like a flame of fire, and His feet like fine brass: I know your works, love, service, faith, and your patience; and as for your works, the last are more than the first. Nevertheless I have a few things against you, because *you allow that woman Jezebel,* who calls herself a prophetess, to teach and seduce My servants to commit sexual immorality and eat things sacrificed to idols. And I gave her time to repent of her sexual immorality, and she did not repent. Indeed I will cast her into a sickbed, and those who commit adultery with her into great tribulation, unless they repent of their deeds. I will kill her children with death, and all the churches shall know that I am He who searches the minds and hearts. And I will give to each one of you according to your works."

—REVELATION 2:18–23, EMPHASIS ADDED

This affirmation and warning from the risen Christ to the church at Thyatira is very similar in tone and content to some of the other prophetic words to the churches that John recorded in chapters 2 and 3 of the Book of Revelation. First of all, the Lord affirmed the Christians for the good things that were operating among them. However, Jesus then gave clear warnings about the need for the churches (most likely by means of their leaders) to expose certain sinful beliefs and practices that were also present. He called the Christians to zealously turn away from such.

The churches of Asia Minor had been partially infiltrated and influenced by some of the false teachers who were circulating about in the first century. This necessary "straight talk" was "tough love" from the Son of God to

His beloved children, who were in danger of bringing divine discipline down upon their own heads. I believe that the churches of our generation need more of this kind of specific, clear exhortation, for similar errors have infiltrated modern Christendom.

In this above passage, Jesus refers to "Jezebel." I believe that there was an actual lady among them who was a false prophetess. However, in using this code name, Jesus was referring to much more than a simple problem with a single person. He was making a direct allusion to the biblical account of Queen Jezebel whom Ahab, the king of Israel in the time of Elijah, took as a wife.

In essence, Christ is saying to these Christians, "Go back and reread the story of Jezebel (1 Kings 16–21; 2 Kings 9), and you will get deeper insight into the nature and scope of the spiritual battle in which you are presently engaged. What happened to Israel in that day is happening among you right now. Learn from the bad example of Ahab and the good (and the not so good!) example of Elijah. The same kind of evil spirit that was working through Queen Jezebel in Israel is working presently in your Christian fellowship. You have made an unholy alliance. Wake up and break its influence—this is no trivial matter. Left unchecked, it has the power to bring sickness, judgment and death upon My church. Deal with it."

Whenever the body of Christ begins to rise up and receive tokens of "the spirit and power of Elijah," it is certain to have a serious confrontation with this "Jezebel spirit" that is firmly established among the nations and even significantly operating within many religious institutions and their political systems. This spirit is content to lay low and cloak its evil until a rival, holy spiritual power comes on the scene and uncovers and challenges

211

it. Let all would-be prophets take special note!

I believe that this spirit is a literal demonic principality of very high rank, but we must seek to demystify significantly how it operates and how it is defeated. Many people get very superstitious about our spiritual warfare. This evil spirit thrives on the panic that emerges from superstition. This is an ancient evil that we are facing, and we don't need some kind of modern spiritual "technological breakthrough" in order to overcome it. It gains its power primarily through the moral and spiritual compromises among God's people. We need a *quiet confidence,* a strong dose of *truth* and a "critical mass" of *right living* among believers to prevail over this evil. We need a *genuine Holy Spirit revival* that simply begins in the inner being of ordinary Christians and church leaders who take their stand for God's righteousness in the gospel of Christ instead of bending in the raging winds of the spirit of this age. If we walk out the gospel and its implications for human life, then God and His mighty angels will work to pull down and displace the unseen demonic stronghold.

We need to look again at the very practical nature of "putting on the whole armor of God," outlined in the last section of Ephesians 6. There's nothing very mysterious or complicated about it. We are plainly called to apply truth, righteousness, the good news of peace in Jesus, faith, the knowledge of salvation, the Word of God and fervent prayer to every arena of human life outlined in the previous chapters of the book—beliefs, attitudes, speech, human relations, sexuality, finances, time management, entertainment, marriage, family and vocation—"to the intent that now the manifold wisdom of God might be made known by the church to the principalities and powers in the heavenly places" (Eph 3:10). What an ingenious way to rebuke the devil. Try it sometime! Try it all the time!

A JEZEBEL SPIRIT

The term "Jezebel spirit" isn't a technical term found in the Bible. However, the characteristics of this *false way of living* are often and clearly described in Scripture. There has been quite a bit of confusion among believers regarding this demonic power. The struggle to pinpoint its nature and methods is part of its very crafty strategy. It is therefore wise to say two things that the Jezebel spirit *is not*.

It is not gender related. It operates through both men and women, young and old. It isn't women with a strong personality and a leadership gift who are still learning to function. Men with a leadership gift, as well as women, will sometimes express themselves inappropriately or too intensely. This has mistakenly been termed a "Jezebel spirit" by some. Such common misuse of the term is spiritually abusive and destructive to sincere, yet immature, believers. We need to have grace to cover all immaturity—which is very different from rebellion.

It is not people who have sincere questions for or conscientious disagreements with church leadership. The Bible values energetic appeals to spiritual authority when needed. (All men and women in true spiritual authority are weak and imperfect people "in process.") Such godly appeals are very different from the mocking and railing against spiritual authority that springs from a Jezebel influence.

Primarily the "Jezebel influence" is a *false way of living,* which a small number of "deluded believers" embrace in a profound way. Many believers may potentially feel their impact, even though this false way is embodied by only a few. Their negative impact causes many believers to lose their confidence in the value and necessity of standing for righteousness. Their godly confidence is shaken by a false fear of being "religious." The presence of this spirit in the community also seeks to cloud and confuse the moral judgment of believers and silence their voice for true righteousness.

The primary characteristics of this sinful way of life include behaviors such as mocking, slandering and reviling spiritual authority; purposeful deceit and manipulation, especially through false prophecy (inventing dreams, visions and words) to control and intimidate people (an actual form of witchcraft); and sexual immorality and seductive behavior.

Further expressions of this same false way of living are described in the following scriptures:

> But there were also false prophets among the people, even as there will be false teachers among you, who will secretly bring in destructive heresies, even denying the Lord who bought them, and bring on themselves swift destruction. And many will follow their destructive ways, because of whom the way of truth will be blasphemed. By covetousness they will exploit you with deceptive words; for a long time their judgment has not been idle, and their destruction does not slumber.
>
> —2 PETER 2:1–3

> ...and especially those who walk according to the flesh in the lust of uncleanness and despise authority. They are presumptuous, self-willed. They are not afraid to speak evil of dignitaries, whereas

angels, who are greater in power and might, do not bring a reviling accusation against them before the Lord. But these, like natural brute beasts made to be caught and destroyed, speak evil of the things they do not understand, and will utterly perish in their own corruption, and will receive the wages of unrighteousness, as those who count it pleasure to carouse in the daytime. They are spots and blemishes, carousing in their own deceptions while they feast with you, having eyes full of adultery and that cannot cease from sin, beguiling unstable souls. They have a heart trained in covetous practices, and are accursed children. They have forsaken the right way and gone astray, following the way of Balaam the son of Beor, who loved the wages of unrighteousness; but he was rebuked for his iniquity: a dumb donkey speaking with a man's voice restrained the madness of the prophet.

—2 PETER 2:10–16

For certain men have crept in unnoticed, who long ago were marked out for this condemnation, ungodly men, who turn the grace of our God into lewdness and deny the only Lord God and our Lord Jesus Christ.

—JUDE 4

But these speak evil of whatever they do not know; and whatever they know naturally, like brute beasts, in these things they corrupt themselves. Woe to them! For they have gone in the way of Cain, have run greedily in the error of Balaam for profit, and perished in the rebellion of Korah. These are spots in your love feasts, while they feast with you without fear, serving only themselves. They are clouds without water, carried about by the winds; late autumn trees without fruit, twice dead, pulled up by the roots; raging waves of the sea, foaming up their own shame; wandering stars for whom is reserved the blackness of darkness forever.

—JUDE 10–13

These are grumblers, complainers, walking according to their own lusts; and they mouth great swelling words, flattering people to gain advantage. But you, beloved, remember the words which were spoken before by the apostles of our Lord Jesus Christ: how they told you that there would be mockers in the last time who would walk according to their own ungodly lusts. These are sensual persons, who cause divisions, not having the Spirit.

—JUDE 16–19

Verse 11 of Jude uses these terms—"the way of Cain" (deep-seated envy and jealousy), "the error of Balaam" (using the spiritual realm for selfish gain) and "the rebellion of Korah" (slander against God-endorsed leadership)—in the same way that Jesus used the term "Jezebel" in Revelation 2. By references to these infamous biblical personalities, we gain insight into the precise nature of the errors and ends of these false teachers who had infiltrated, mostly unnoticed, the Christian community. The main damage they did was to twist subtly the doctrine of *God's grace into licentiousness*—that is, their false teaching served to condone sin (Jude 4).

These teachers were influential, credible, crafty and skilled in religious rhetoric and twisting the Scriptures. Their arrogance was commonly expressed in cynical mocking of spiritual authority. They confidently presented themselves as having genuine prophetic anointing as they sought recognition and preeminence. The fruit of their ways was always divisive. God was then reluctantly obligated by His just nature to bring corresponding just disciplines and judgments to bear upon His own people. Today, just as then, this breaks His heart and grieves His Spirit.

There is a threefold false confidence that results within the overall church community when such evil is tolerated.

- *A false confidence* to engage in "socially acceptable" dabbling with immorality, drunkenness and moral compromise. This comes from promoting the idea that you're "religious" if you are concerned about biblical standards of righteousness.

- *A false confidence* to lie, for example, by adding "a little to the truth" in reporting conjured-up information supposedly received by the Holy Spirit. This counterfeit self-induced "prophetic revelation" is regularly used without any shame or fear of God.

- *A false confidence* to mock and rail against spiritual authority, which results in confusion and division within the body.

What we are facing today in the body of Christ is nothing new or unusual. These sins are common to the flesh of humans and the spirit of this fallen age. It's nothing to "freak out" about! The very same deceptions that crop up here and there around the body of Christ were present in the first-century church. It has been well said that there really are no *new* heresies. The issue is whether we will have the discernment and courage to free ourselves and our communities of faith from this false form of pseudoreligion.

SHOWING MERCY WITH FEAR

On a final note, we must deal wisely and lovingly with individual people who may have fallen prey to this kind of spiritual deception. There are people in different stages of being influenced by this false way. Some are weak in faith, and doubts are plaguing them. We should approach them gently and give them a lot of mercy and time to think and work through their issues. Others are more deeply entrenched in the deception and need to be dealt with more urgently and radically. Still others have become purveyors of the false teaching, and we must take a stand against them for the sake of the threat that these false teachers pose to the larger body of believers. These three broad categories are clearly referred to by Jude in the specific context of ministering to people specifically under the influence of this error:

> And have mercy on some, who are doubting; save others, snatching them out of the fire; and on some have mercy with fear, hating even the garment polluted by the flesh.
>
> —JUDE 22–23, NAS

Finally, as we face situations with specific people, we should heed the advice of Paul to Timothy, who also had the difficult task of keeping his congregation free from various errors and heresies:

> But avoid foolish and ignorant disputes, knowing that they generate strife. And a servant of the Lord must not quarrel but be gentle to all, able to teach, patient, in humility correcting those who are in opposition, if God perhaps will grant them repentance, so that they may know the truth, and that they may come to their senses and escape the snare of the devil, having been taken captive by him to do his will.
>
> —2 TIMOTHY 2:23–26

Essentially, Paul says to Timothy, "Don't quarrel, but be gentle, patient, discerning and humble in your dealings with these people—maybe God will deliver these demonically deceived and estranged brothers and sisters. There's always hope."

Chapter 12

THE FUTURE OF
PROPHETIC MINISTRY

T HE PROPHECY FROM Joel 2, which Peter quoted on the day of Pentecost (it has been mentioned several times in this book), is a major key to understanding the future of the body of Christ. It is one of many Old Testament prophecies that have multiple fulfillments.

VISIONS, DREAMS, WONDERS AND SIGNS

But this is what was spoken by the prophet Joel: "And it shall come to pass in the last days, says God, that I will pour out of My Spirit on all flesh; your sons and your daughters shall prophesy, your young men shall see visions, your old men shall dream dreams. And on My menservants and on My maidservants I will pour out My Spirit in those days; and they shall prophesy. I will show wonders in heaven above and signs in the earth beneath: blood and fire and vapor of smoke. The sun shall be turned into darkness, and the moon into blood, before the coming of the great and awesome day of the LORD. And it shall come to pass that whoever calls on the name of the LORD shall be saved."

—ACTS 2:16–21

This prophecy follows a well-known and historically established hermeneutical principle of Bible prophecy interpretation. This prophecy, and others like it, had a "historical-grammatical" fulfillment, a first-century fulfillment and an "eschatological" (Last Days) fulfillment. Some of them even find elements of their ultimate fulfillment in the age to come.

By the inspiration of the Holy Spirit, Peter understood that this divine visitation at Pentecost was a fulfillment of Joel's prophecy. This is without question. However, by examining the content of the prophecy, we can clearly deduce that it was not fulfilled totally in the first century. There are definite eschatological aspects of this prophecy that have yet to take place in world history. Yet, these things will all come to pass *before* the Second Coming of Christ. I do not believe in the *immediate return* of Jesus because of my expectation that these prophecies will be fulfilled in this age. However, I do believe in the *imminent return* of Jesus, and once these End-Time prophecies begin to happen, they will happen very quickly. "For He will finish the work and cut it short in righteousness, because the Lord will make a *short work* upon the earth" (Rom. 9:28, emphasis added).

This leads us to some exciting conclusions about the future of the body of Christ, the expression of Christianity that will characterize the Last-Day church and the mighty acts of God that will be demonstrated in those days. "Great and terrible" are good adjectives for the "day of the Lord" that is often spoken about in the Scriptures. It will be "great" for the saints of God and "terrible" for all who have not obeyed the gospel of Jesus Christ!

It is notable that the main manifestation of the global outpouring of the Holy Spirit upon the last generation of believers is the prophetic ministry. It will come upon the old and the young—male and female alike. The unstated, but clearly implied, ramification of this spiritual power, which will rest upon believers in general, relates to the heavenly wonders and the earthly signs referred to in the prophecy. Specifically, it is the spirit of prophecy upon all believers that connects the outpouring of the Spirit and the cataclysmic events of the last part of the prophecy. I believe that God intends to use *human vessels* to prophesy about the timing, nature and location of many of these signs—just as He used Moses in the release of His specifically foretold judgments upon Egypt. Likewise, God used Elijah, a man with weaknesses like all human vessels, to prophesy heavenly wonders and earthly signs—the stopping of rain and fire coming down to earth out of heaven.

This level of prophetic power also will be demonstrated through the ministry of the two witnesses in Revelation 11.

> "And I will give power to my two witnesses, and they will prophesy one thousand two hundred and sixty days, clothed in sackcloth." These are the two olive trees and the two lampstands standing before the God of the earth. And if anyone wants to harm them, fire proceeds from their mouth and devours

their enemies. And if anyone wants to harm them, he must be killed in this manner. These have power to shut heaven, so that no rain falls in the days of their prophecy; and they have power over waters to turn them to blood, and to strike the earth with all plagues, as often as they desire.

—Revelation 11:3–6

Although I believe that the two witnesses are literally two people, the "spirit and power of Elijah" that will be upon them will generally rest upon the whole body of Christ in those days. This is what Joel's prophecy alludes to. The scenario that Scripture depicts for the final generation includes wonders and judgments reminiscent of the Book of Exodus, and healings and miracles reminiscent of the Book of Acts. The divine melodrama of those days, however, will far outstrip the mighty acts He performed in either of those two generations. The very last days will be *Exodus plus Acts to the second power!* It will not be simply Moses vs. Pharaoh on a local Egyptian stage or the apostles vs. the first-century Jewish rulers on a local Jerusalem stage. It will be a "power encounter" of the highest magnitude between the forces of good and evil. Each will crescendo to the height of fully matured manifestations of power. It will be a clash between the mighty End-Time church, filled with unprecedented spiritual power, vs. the Antichrist and his satanically inspired and empowered forces—layed out on an international, cosmic stage. This spiritual war will climax with the bodily return of Jesus Christ from heaven with all His saints and angelic hosts. He will slay the Antichrist with the "breath of His mouth" and "the brightness of His coming" (2 Thess. 2:8).

PROPHETIC ETIQUETTE

REMODELING THE PROPHETIC MINISTRY

I am presently involved in helping to lead a prophetic team ministry called *Shiloh Ministries International*. The catalyst for this ministry, on the human end, is Paul Cain. He has been serving the body of Christ with a prophetic ministry of integrity and purity for over fifty years. Paul moved to Kansas City in 1996 to establish this new ministry thrust. Paul has a desire and a divine commission to mentor people who have been sovereignly called by God to the prophetic ministry, in addition to touching spiritual, business and political leaders through the profound revelatory ministry that God has entrusted to him.

The Lord recently impressed upon Paul that there is a different kind of *model* for prophetic ministry that the Holy Spirit desires for us to embrace. He is challenging us to discern it and pass it on to others as He leads us. Although we aren't presuming that we have fully understood this different model as of yet, we do know that it revolves around a *higher quality* of prophetic revelation coming forth in contrast to a *greater quantity* of prophetic words being given. We also think it involves a greater amount of work "behind the scenes" than on public platforms. The Holy Spirit is presently challenging us, in the spirit of Proverbs 25:2, to seek out this matter that God is presently concealing from us to some degree:

> It is the glory of God to conceal a matter, but the glory of kings is to search out a matter.
> —PROVERBS 25:2

One of my dearest friends and my prayer partner in

224

Shiloh's ministry is Terry Bennett. His quality of life in the Spirit and in prophetic ministry is a constant inspiration and challenge to me. He is significantly modeling the kind of prophetic life and ministry that I suspect God is calling Shiloh to promote within the body of Christ in the days ahead. Recently, Terry had a powerful vision that we both believe directly relates to this new prophetic ministry model.

In this vision, Terry saw the Lord was remodeling His house (the body of Christ), much like a carpenter would. He began with the kitchen cabinets (a word play on traditional styles of prophetic leadership, as "kitchen cabinet" is a term sometimes used to refer to the leaders around a president). Terry intuitively knew that the kitchen was the room in the house that represented the prophetic ministry. The Lord was ripping out the cabinets and throwing away the old canned food that was within them (a word picture for some of the ineffective traditional teachings about and practices of the prophetic ministry). This food was well past its expiration date and even dangerous to eat. Terry knew that the rebuilding the Lord was intending to do in this kitchen and the food that He was going to restock in the new cabinets would be of a quality that would amaze and greatly bless the body of Christ.

I believe that the kind of prophetic power the Lord intends to release in and through the body of Christ has hardly begun to show itself in the earth. So far, we have just been "scratching the surface" of prophetic ministry.

A Pathway for Prophetic People

In 1990, I had a remarkable prophetic experience. The

message that God gave me has become a part of my life message in God's service to the body of Christ. Early one morning, suddenly and without notice, the power of the Holy Spirit descended upon my body as I was lying in bed. I actually fell into a trance. (People can typically see or hear into the spiritual realm distinctly when the Holy Spirit causes them to experience a trance.) At one point in this encounter with the Lord, I heard an audible voice speak to me, saying, "Isaiah 50." After coming out of this trance, I went to get my Bible, and to my astonishment my marker was actually placed in this very chapter. At that point in my life, I really had no idea what Isaiah 50 was all about. As I looked down upon the chapter, my eyes immediately landed upon verse 4: "The Lord GOD has given Me the tongue of the learned, that I should know how to speak a word in season to him who is weary. He awakens Me morning by morning, He awakens My ear to hear as the learned."

I realized that this was an exact description of what I had just experienced—God had "awakened my ear" in the morning.

As I have meditated upon this chapter, I believe that the Lord has given me a message to the body of Christ regarding the Christian experience in general and the prophetic pathway in particular.

> Thus says the LORD: "Where is the certificate of your mother's divorce, whom I have put away? Or which of My creditors is it to whom I have sold you? For your iniquities you have sold yourselves, and for your transgressions your mother has been put away. Why, when I came, was there no man? Why, when I called, was there none to answer? Is My hand shortened at

all that it cannot redeem? Or have I no power to deliver? Indeed with My rebuke I dry up the sea, I make the rivers a wilderness; their fish stink because there is no water, and die of thirst. I clothe the heavens with blackness, and I make sackcloth their covering."

"The Lord GOD has given Me the tongue of the learned, that I should know how to speak a word in season to him who is weary. He awakens Me morning by morning, He awakens My ear to hear as the learned. The Lord GOD has opened My ear; and I was not rebellious, nor did I turn away. I gave My back to those who struck Me, and My cheeks to those who plucked out the beard; I did not hide My face from shame and spitting.

For the Lord GOD will help Me; therefore I will not be disgraced; therefore I have set My face like a flint, and I know that I will not be ashamed. He is near who justifies Me; who will contend with Me? Let us stand together. Who is My adversary? Let him come near Me. Surely the Lord GOD will help Me; who is he who will condemn Me? Indeed they will all grow old like a garment; the moth will eat them up.

"Who among you fears the LORD? Who obeys the voice of His Servant? Who walks in darkness and has no light? Let him trust in the name of the LORD and rely upon his God. Look, all you who kindle a fire, who encircle yourselves with sparks: walk in the light of your fire and in the sparks you have kindled—this you shall have from My hand: you shall lie down in torment."

—ISAIAH 50:1–11

I identify this passage by three phrases: *the invitation to intimacy, the inevitability of suffering* and *the essentiality of dependency.* The passage begins with a heart cry from God over the breach in His relationship to His children caused by the spiritual defection of His "wife" and their "mother"—the Jewish nation as a whole. God did not "divorce her" or have to "sell her" because of poverty. *She* forsook and divorced *Him.* The nation came under a necessary judgment for its sin against God, who cannot deny His just nature.

God then asks if the relational problem has to do with His lack of power. Of course it doesn't. God is not short on *power,* but He has often been short on *partners.* One of the amazing points of theological truth throughout all Scripture is God's desire and passion to have voluntary human partners in His kingdom purposes. This vital reality has so often been overlooked, minimized and rationalized away in the history of both Israel and the church. This is a point of truth that the prophetic ministries among God's people have often been called to highlight. God had looked for human intercessors to respond to His initiatives, but no one showed up to stand in the gap.

In the void created by this spiritual defection, God mercifully takes the matter into His own capable hands. Since no one was found to intercede, His own arm brings His salvation. The "servant of the Lord" appears on the scene in verse 4. In the Book of Isaiah, this is first and foremost a reference to the Messiah Himself. However, it is also a reference to the Israel of God in a corporate sense. Here, it is a prophetic picture of Israel, spiritually restored and freshly anointed, living up to and fulfilling her prophetic identity and destiny. This is a common theme throughout Isaiah. Therefore it is consistent to

The Future of Prophetic Ministry

apply these principles not only to Jesus, but also to the people of God in any generation—and especially the body of Christ. Christians are called to follow the Servant of the Lord and to be servants of the Lord according to the same Spirit.

The Servant boasts in how the Lord God has graciously granted Him the tongue of a learned one who moves in the prophetic—speaking a "word in season" to the weary. What a beautiful description of the genuine purpose of prophetic ministry! But notice, there is a secret to this anointed speech that precedes it. This is the "awakened ear" that is opened to hear the Lord and to learn directly from Him. In prophetic ministry, anointed *listening* is fundamental to anointed *speaking!* This is the *invitation to intimacy* that the Lord is issuing to believers far and wide in our day.

The Servant of the Lord has had His ear opened, and yet now He is testifying about how He "was not rebellious." How does the temptation to rebellion fit in with this intimate love affair between the Servant and the voice of God? God will woo us by His sweet and tender voice into the prophetic, and then He will tell us things to believe and do that can often get us into a "heap of trouble" with the people of the earth who don't "give a rip" about what He has to say! But the Servant has been divinely ambushed—He is already "lovesick for God," and it's too late to back out.

This is the *inevitability of suffering*. We won't get out of this thing with our comfort zones intact. God is graciously making it so that our comfort zones are no longer comfortable—this is a severe mercy. We will be tested in the fires of false accusation and persecution. However, the Lord will meet us in that place and stand beside us to strengthen us to endure whatever may come against us.

Paul quotes parts of verses 6–9 of Isaiah 50 in that great chapter of Christian victory—Romans 8.

Verses 10–11 of Isaiah 50 speak of the *essentiality of dependency*. Isaiah is challenging us about our fidelity to our Master—the ultimate Servant of the Lord—Jesus Christ. He declares that we "walk in darkness and have no light." However, this is not *moral darkness* as in the book of 1 John. It is *circumstantial darkness*—the ordinary backdrop of a life of obedience to God, even for prophetic people! This dynamic is designed by God to evoke our trust and dependency upon Him. The darkness demands dependency. This quality of deep trust of God in uncertainty is the definition of spiritual maturity, and God will grant us plenty of opportunities to discover if we possess it.

One of His favorite dealings in this hour with His prophetically called servants is "dangling." He is displacing them from their positions, titles, job descriptions, human relationships, organizations and financial securities through divine disruptions and allowing them to "not know" for a while what He is asking of them for the next season. This dealing centers around breaking off a wrong "control spirit" over their own lives. (This is not the same as the moral "self-control" that is a fruit of the Spirit.)

Finally, Isaiah warn us about "kindling our own fires" when God is testing us in the darkness. Let us not turn to the arm of the flesh or to self-reliance in such a season of divine dangling—this is the worst possible thing that we can do. Our loving and firm Father will discipline us for such carnal antics. Just go limp and find the peace of God. This will prepare you most fully to be directly led into the next appointed season and assignment.

These are specific elements of and a divine pathway for how God is preparing His prophetic vessels for the melodramatic days ahead on Planet Earth.

THE PRIESTLY, PROPHETIC AND KINGLY PROGRESSION

> But Samuel ministered before the LORD, even as a child, wearing a linen ephod.
>
> —1 SAMUEL 2:18

> And the child Samuel grew in stature, and in favor both with the LORD and men.
>
> —1 SAMUEL 2:26

> Now the LORD came and stood and called as at other times, "Samuel! Samuel!" And Samuel answered, "Speak, for Your servant hears."
>
> —1 SAMUEL 3:10

> So Samuel grew, and the LORD was with him and let none of his words fall to the ground. And all Israel from Dan to Beersheba knew that Samuel had been established as a prophet of the LORD. Then the LORD appeared again in Shiloh. For the LORD revealed Himself to Samuel in Shiloh by the word of the LORD.
>
> —1 SAMUEL 3:19–21

Samuel's life is an excellent picture of the kind of quality prophetic ministry that the Lord Jesus is zealous to bring forth in this hour among believers. Before he was a *prophet* or a *judge* who anointed *kings*, he was a priest whose priority, even from his youth, was to *minister to the Lord*.

231

When we *wait* on the Lord, we aren't just *waiting* for the Lord to act while we fold our arms, tap our foot impatiently and look at our watch in frustration. No, we minister to the Lord and extravagantly pour out upon Him our love, gratitude, intercessions, supplications (prayer to the second power!), praises and affection—and our precious time, money and energies. We do this in the light of who He is, what He has done and what He has yet promised to do. He doesn't need anything from us, but He does desire to be desperately wanted and sought after—just as any lover does. There are things that we can give (sacrifice) to God that bring Him pleasure. What an honor and what dignity we have as priests (in the New Testament concept of the "priesthood of every believer") of the Lord.

> You also, as living stones, are being built up a spiritual house, a holy priesthood, to offer up spiritual sacrifices acceptable to God through Jesus Christ.
>
> —1 PETER 2:5

> Therefore by Him let us continually offer the sacrifice of praise to God, that is, the fruit of our lips, giving thanks to His name. But do not forget to do good and to share, for with such sacrifices God is well pleased.
>
> —HEBREWS 13:15–16

Samuel was caught up into the love and worship of God, and then the Lord responded to his faith (and his mother's) and ultimately, undeniably established him as a prophet in the nation. Samuel's anointing and accuracy became so great that *"none* of his words fell to the ground."

God is going to be calling many men and women aside

to seek Him in secret and hidden ways. Those who will apprehend the grace to respond to this priestly invitation will find their delight in being "before the Lord." In that context of intimacy and delight, in time, God will begin to share some of His secrets with them. They will not even be allowed to publicly share many of the insights and experiences into which God will lead them. However, they will be commissioned to share a portion of these prophetic revelations with the body of Christ, and those words will have the power within them to change the very "chemistry" of human lives and relationships for the glory of God. This quality of "priestly ministry" will set the stage for a higher caliber of "prophetic ministry" than we have seen heretofore in the church.

I have some marvelous friends who are significantly arranging and rearranging their lives and lifestyles to embrace this kind of divine invitation. I won't say more about them for fear of "blowing their cover," but it is sufficient just to say that the Lord is quickly (in just a few short years) meeting them and granting a prophetic quality to their lives that is sometimes stunning.

I believe that there is, in general, a divine progression for Christian influence in the earth. At its best, it follows a pattern from priestly ministry to prophetic ministry to kingly ministry. If people have a mind to try to skip over one dimension in an attempt to push their way into another, then they ultimately will not find the center of God's will and will be unnecessarily spiritually thwarted in many ways. *Priestly ministry* is about loving on the Lord and quietly serving others for His sake and reward alone. Mature *prophetic ministry* simply involves a divine response in which the Holy Spirit regularly entrusts divine revelation to such humble "priests" of the Lord. (I am not referring here to an official title or position in the eyes of people, but to men and women, married and single, both old and young who are ordinary workers in the market-place and members of regular families throughout the earth that have it in their hearts to seek the Lord.) He is "a rewarder of those who diligently seek him" (Heb 11:6). *Kingly ministry* is a calling that manifests in various mea-sures—from family, to families, to church, to churches, to city, to cities, to region, to nation, to nations. It relates to and operates by the exercising of spiritual authority to *move* both the invisible and visible realms. It can move people to action by the moral force of wise and simple words, and it can move sicknesses and demons that are hindering God's purposes out of the way.

We must be willing and joyful to minister humbly to the Lord as priests. This is fundamental to the other dimen-sions of service to God, and it is ongoing in nature. We may become rightly occupied with prophetic and kingly duties, but we must always remain *preoccupied* with the responsibility, privilege and pleasure of loving on and seeking the Lord Himself. As Mike Bickle has so often said, "God is restoring the *first commandment to first place.*"

PROPHETIC MENTORING

My experience of moving into the initial phases of a prophetic ministry has been instructive to many of my friends and students at the Grace Training Center of Kansas City. I am including it in this book in the hope that it will likewise give insight to others who read about it. I cannot avoid drawing attention to Paul Cain in the process. Through a number of God-ordered interactions with him, and by divine providence, Paul has become a spiritual father and mentor to me. It is sometimes a fine line between drawing too much attention to the human vessels whom God so powerfully uses in our lives and properly giving honor to whom it is due. Fortunately, Paul can handle the praise because he seems to be more aware of his human weakness than anyone I know. Anyone who has heard him knows that he speaks about his frailties openly.

I believe that *mentoring* is going to become a very important divine strategy and educational model for the proper and healthy propagation of the kind of prophetic ministry for which the Lord Jesus is jealous. God is raising up spiritual fathers and mothers who are going to be enabled to pour their experience and knowledge into the lives of younger men and women who are hungry to learn. We will be able to help them avoid many mistakes and thereby minimize the trials they will have to endure. God intends to join the generations together in a wonderful way for His glory to be seen among the nations and for the furtherance of His kingdom in this crucial generation. My wife's journey and my own journey into prophetic ministry demonstrate this mentoring principle.

As I have spoken about in detail in earlier chapters, as a young person I experienced the power of the Holy Spirit in my relationship with the Lord. At age sixteen I heard the internally audible voice of God. I was convicted of my sins through this dramatic encounter. Two years later, I surrendered my will to Jesus Christ and asked Him into my life after an intense two-week period during which the Spirit was supernaturally confronting me and drawing me to Him. I had two prophetic visions in the very moment I prayed to receive Christ.

A week later I was filled with the Holy Spirit as I sat inside my home praying. I didn't fully understand what was happening to me as the Spirit suddenly and powerfully came upon me. I hadn't even been asking for such a thing to happen. An insatiable hunger to read the Bible overtook me, and I often experienced supernatural illumination as I read. A year later, I had my first spiritual dream. It was about sharing my faith with a friend from high school. The next day, in obedience to the dream, I went to see her, and she accepted Jesus as soon as I shared the gospel with her.

Over the next four years, many of my college friends at Miami University in Oxford, Ohio, accepted the Lord, and a true spirit of revival touched our campus. Several hundred students were converted and filled with the Spirit through this work of God. I was raised up, to my surprise, to become the leader of this Spirit-filled student fellowship, and the Spirit of the Lord anointed me to preach and teach with authority. We saw marvelous answers to prayer and more than a few undeniable miracles.

After marrying my wife, Terri, who had been a part of our campus fellowship, we left Ohio and moved to Arkansas to plant and pastor churches. Eight years later, we moved to Michigan to carry on our ministry. In 1987 we were suddenly sent to Kansas City to join the leadership team of what is now Metro Christian Fellowship. The first three of our children, Luke, Lisa and Samuel, were born in Arkansas. Michael and Stephen came along after we moved to Kansas City.

In the years that followed the campus revival, I began to experience a "slow leak" of the fullness of the Spirit I had once known and enjoyed. More and more I began to rely on my intellectual powers in the dispensing of my ministry to God's people. From time to time I would suspect that something like this was occurring. However, I would brush those nagging thoughts aside and double my efforts to serve God with zeal. At times, God would graciously intervene in my growing family's life and give us another taste of His powerful presence. Still, this "leaking out" continued until I became a significantly burdened, relationally heavy, boring, legalistic, religious, weary and dried-up believer and preacher.

During this thirteen-year period, the "oil" in the lamp of my ministry had run out, and only the dry "wick" was there to burn—creating the smoke and smell that was not only filling my eyes and nose, but also the eyes and noses of the people around me. By 1990 my wife and children weren't even getting the leftovers of my spiritual, emotional and physical energy—even they had been depleted!

In May of 1990, a marvelous divine breakthrough was initiated in my life that is carrying on to this day. God used Paul Cain in quite a dramatic fashion to speak to my heart and expose my spiritual predicament. In 1988, after hearing me minister publicly, Paul had prophesied privately to me concerning a wonderful divine promise and challenge. He said, "Michael, the Lord has a wonderful future for you here in Kansas City. You have many things in your heart to share with the body of Christ. Just make sure you aim for the heart and not for the head." I took this word from God to heart as it mysteriously confirmed some deep longings within me, but I didn't fully understand what the Lord was saying to me through it.

On this night in May of 1990, God stirred Paul to speak a prophetic word to me for the first time in public. A few days before this word was given, in concert with my coworkers, it had been decided that I should step back from my regular preaching and teaching ministry in our fellowship. This was due to the conviction within our leadership team that God had not recently been "blessing" my preaching and teaching to our church body. That was a kind way of stating that my preaching was "stinking up the place!" In reality, God was temporarily lifting His hand off my public ministry. This had been confusing and frustrating to me—sometimes downright humiliating. I had been hoping that no one would notice—but everyone did. Paul had come to town that May, not knowing anything about our decision. He delivered the following word to us:

> Michael and Terri, I asked the Lord to give me a promise for your life because I happen to know that you're going through a transition. The Lord gave me Isaiah 30:15: "In quietness and confidence shall be your strength." The Lord is showing you that if you will come away and rest for a while, a new fresh breeze will blow into your life and blow away all the dross and all the things that would keep you from being the fiery, anointed messenger that the Lord wants to make of you. The prophetic person and the prophetic quality the Lord is giving you needs time and quietness to build confidence and strength. Rest assured that what is happening in this transition time is truly for your good—for both of you and for your family. This is not in any way the Lord putting you down; it's the Lord showing you a way whereby He can actually, in due time, exalt Himself in you to the ultimate glory of the Father. Just rest in that, and confidence will build. Another scripture for you is: "Do not cast away your confi-

dence, which has great reward" (Heb. 10:35). Don't cast away any of that faith. It's going to pay off. There's going to be some real inner peace, new commitments and new direction for your life that is more fulfilling than you've ever dreamed of in any other place—including this particular vocation you may be stepping away from. Now God will surely visit you, give you peace, give you strength and your soul will prosper abundantly, outlandishly. When you're filled and refilled you will come again rejoicing in greater power than you had before.

At that time, no one but Terri and I knew that Isaiah 30:15 ("In returning and rest you shall be saved; in quietness and confidence shall be your strength") was a "life verse" that God had given to each of us before we even knew one another. Neither did anyone know the depth to which my confidence in ministry had been shaken. There is no way to describe to anyone the profound nature of this prophetic word and the impact that it has had on our lives. God looked down upon me with pity in His heart. In that moment, He clearly exposed my condition to my family, my whole church family and to me. He revealed His diagnosis of my spiritual sickness and His promise of a remedy for it. It "hurt so good!"

Later that night I was up praying, unable to sleep. As I knelt in prayer in my living room, I saw a very clear vision in my mind's eye that surprised and almost amused me. I saw Charlton Heston in his portrayal of Moses in the movie *The Ten Commandments*. It was the scene where he is coming down the mountain after being in God's presence for many days. Even his physical countenance had been changed through this divine encounter.

I knew immediately what the Holy Spirit was showing me, and I prayed a secret prayer, "Lord, I want to go to the Rocky Mountains and become a different man."

I never revealed this vision or request to anyone except Terri. A month or so later, our leadership team was reviewing the prophecy that Paul had given to us that night in May. They all agreed, without my mentioning one word, that I should go away from Kansas City for a while. Within a few days, without my "lifting a finger," arrangements had been made for my whole family to spend the whole month of August 1990 in beautiful accommodations in the Rocky Mountains at no financial expense to us.

After the thirteen-hour drive, on that first night in Breckenridge, Colorado, as I lay my head upon the pillow to sleep I had a powerful spiritual dream. The next night I had another. The night after, I had two more. I experienced about thirty spiritual dreams in those thirty days—undoubtedly a direct reference to the Isaiah 30 passage given to us by Paul Cain in the prophecy. These dreams were of a quality and clarity I had only experienced a handful of times in my whole Christian life. Each morning for a few hours I would walk the mountain pathways and meditate on the Book of Psalms. Terri would take at least a couple of hours each afternoon and spend time in solitude with the Lord while I entertained our four young children. Each day we also spent time together as a family having fun and seeing the glorious sights that those Rocky Mountain towns and countryside provide. Something good and invigorating was soaking into me and settling upon me, something of heaven—a kiss from God upon my weary soul.

After returning home, a number of people remarked to me how different I seemed to be—even physically. At the time, I never connected this to my vision of Moses and my prayer on the night that the prophecy was delivered to me. Then, at the beginning of October, Paul Cain came back to town. Before preaching that night, he began to speak about how he had prayed for our leadership team. Then he turned, pointed to Terri and me and prophesied to us once again:

> But Michael doesn't need much prayer. Your thirty days with the Lord really paid off. You came back with your face shining. Everyone else knew it even though you didn't. The revelations of the Lord are with you in a wonderful way, and He's just waiting to give you the application. He's taken the desire out of your heart to reach the mind of man. Now He's given you a way to reach the heart of man. And it's not on the intellectual level—it's on the charismatic, revelatory level. So I see many, many visions and dreams coming to both of you. Terri, you're included, too.

Paul had known nothing in the natural about my thirty-day sabbatical. No one but I knew of the vision I had received. And yet the Lord had shown Paul this very picture for me. Neither did anyone know that Terri and I had a disagreement after the first prophecy had been given. Terri thought that parts of it had applied to her life as well as to mine. I contended that it only applied to me. Now in the second prophecy, the Lord made very clear who had been correct—and it wasn't me! The prophetic ministry is truly amazing when it exposes the secrets of human hearts and private conversations.

Since this time, Terri and I have been growing in our experience with the prophetic ministry of the Holy Spirit.

We had to become like children all over again as we attempted to learn this new direction in our lives and ministries. The dreams and visions have continued with us with a dynamic like the ebbing and flowing of ocean tides. Gradually, the Spirit began to add more "words of knowledge" to our prophetic package.

The Lord Jesus has continued to deal with me gently, but firmly, in this area of overrelying upon my intellect and my human zeal. From time to time, this has continued to be a detriment to my personal relationships and the dispensing of my ministry. Time and time again I have learned that the Lord's ways are profoundly different from mine. He tolerates things that disgust me and is often grieved over things that I tolerate. There have been times when I was convinced that the negative energy I felt rising in my heart over certain situations was the "jealousy of God" moving within me. Only later would I discover that it was my own religious zeal in operation—not the mind of Christ. As I have sought the Lord for deeper insight on this matter, He has gradually been giving me a subjective discernment between the temptations of religious spirits and the influence of the Holy Spirit. There is a religious kind of intolerance that disguises itself as a love for the truth—of which I have been guilty on many occasions in the past.

In 1994, Paul gave me another public prophecy that directly addressed this issue in my life. This was his word:

> Michael, the Lord has given you a great call to leadership. I've written down an impression here that you've been very loyal to that calling. But here you are again in another transition. Don't be too surprised at what the Lord may do for you. Now this is not a

rebuke—it seems like every time I call you out it sounds like a rebuke. But there's something that I just need to say here. You have such a strong revelatory ministry that sometimes you may be too firm—or come across as too firm. So with mercy and compassion the Lord wants you to speak the truth in love. It will be "bismuth"—it will be smooth. The Lord will just bring real healing to your family and your life. God bless you, Michael, and your dear family.

Bismuth is the active ingredient in Pepto-Bismol that calms indigestion. Apparently, the way that I was ministering the word of God was sometimes creating spiritual indigestion in people!

The next day I had a follow-up conversation with Paul regarding this word. He elaborated on the insight that the Spirit of God had given to him for me. The adjustment the Lord was bringing me had to do with my need to show more freely the love and compassion that did actually exist within my heart for people. I needed to be more emotionally engaging and warm and less "monotone" in my delivery of God's word to people. Also, he had an impression that a situation with a person whom I had recently attempted to correct, about which he knew nothing in the natural, had been wounding to her because I had overlooked the sincerity in her heart before the Lord. I was amazed and deeply convicted because the Spirit of God had revealed my confrontation with this person to Paul. Again, the gift of prophecy was revealing and exposing the secrets of my heart.

Even as we were interacting that day, Paul remembered that he had had a dream of him delivering to me the phrase coined by John Wesley: "Love can be murdered by the truth." This truth applied to me, and in the dream I had received the correction well. Paul told me that day that I had received well the first correction he had given me about "aiming for the heart," and that I have been blessed and given more spiritual authority each time that I have received corrections like this from the Lord. He then spoke to me about "maligning"—telling the truth about someone or even to someone with the intention of hurting them. He warned me, by implication, about this temptation in my life. He cautioned me that I must be very careful in situations in which I am called to speak a truth that has a potential of being hurtful to people.

Paul was mentoring me in the prophetic. So often we want to hear a "good word" from a prophetic person, and I have received quite a few. However, I have to say that I benefited most from the loving words of prophetic correction that have come from a true spiritual father.

Many times I have prayed to the Lord out of the following two scriptures:

> Let the righteous strike me; it shall be a kindness. And let him rebuke me; it shall be as excellent oil; let my head not refuse it. For still my prayer is against the deeds of the wicked.
> —Psalm 141:5

> For the commandment is a lamp, and the law a light; reproofs of instruction are the way of life.
> —Proverbs 6:23

If the devil can't successfully keep us from becoming Christians, he will typically try one of two strategies. Either he will attempt to bring us into the bondage of the sins of the flesh or into the bondage of the more "refined" sins of the spirit—religious sins. Both will keep us from becoming effective and powerful believers. These religious sins generally manifest in arenas such as legalism, self-righteousness, divisiveness or judgmentalism. These sins of the spirit are subtler in nature and can easily creep un-awares into believer's hearts over time if we are not alert and vigilant to guard ourselves against their encroachment.

Facing this historical, sinful imbalance between truth and love in my life has become one of my greatest challenges. From time to time, I have significantly wounded the people I love the most, as well as others, because of this negative "stronghold" in my soul. Little by little the Spirit of the Lord is helping me to surmount and over-come this imbalance and become more like our Lord Jesus, who is full of both grace and truth.

THE SEAL OF GENUINENESS

In 1992 our church was having its first Sunday night cele-bration service for all of our related congregations in the Kansas City area. There were about eighteen hundred people present, and they seemed very excited about meeting with the Lord that night. Our worship leader opened the evening, and as he struck the first chord of the first worship song, it was as though a giant wet blanket descended upon whole congregation at once! It wasn't just a dead service underway—it was doubly dead! Jeff fumbled his way through that first song, but midway through the second song he stopped and turned around to the leaders on the platform. He said in confusion and frustration, "I can't do this."

Mike Bickle came to the podium and informed the

congregation that something was going on that we didn't understand. He encouraged everyone to greet and visit with one another for a while as the leaders put their heads together to figure out what to do. It was obvious to everyone that something unusual was taking place, and we assumed and hoped that the Lord had something specific in mind to accomplish. We could surely tell that the enemy did!

Mike asked all of the leaders if any of us had any kind of prophetic inspiration to share with the congregation. Both Jim Goll, a dear friend with an established prophetic ministry, and I did, in fact, have some prophetic stirrings going on within us at the time. Mike said to us, "I guess you're on." When we called everyone back together, Jim got up and shared how the Lord was desirous of cleansing the prophetic womb of our church and that we had pulled back too far into fear on the heels of the international controversy that had swirled around our ministry over the previous two years. He said that the Lord wanted to restore us to place of responsiveness to the Spirit of prophecy.

At that point I came to the podium. There were two words that were upon my heart that night. The first was a passage of Scripture that describes the nature of the evidences of genuine New Testament Christianity. I applied this passage to our lives and to the future of the body of Christ in this generation.

I had brought a book to the podium with me called *Some Said It Thundered* by David Pytches. This book had been written by this wonderful Spirit-filled Anglican bishop and had become a bestseller in Europe over the previous couple of years. It was an account of the prophetic history of our fellowship and some of the supernatural events that accompanied our beginning. Mike Bickle and I referred to

246

some of these testimonies in our book *Growing in the Prophetic,* also published by Creation House.

A few weeks prior to this celebration meeting, I had felt that the Lord revealed something to me that seemed rather odd to me at the time. It related to an American bishop who back in the 1960s wrote a book about communicating with his deceased son through the use of a medium. His last name also ended with a "P." The account of this occultic activity seemed to spread like wildfire across our nation at that time. Even as an unchurched little boy I remembered hearing about it. What the Spirit had said to me was, "There was a 'Bishop P' who opened the door to the church world for the false prophetic. But I have my own 'Bishop P' who will open the door to the church world for the true prophetic."

As I was reporting this strong prophetic impression to the congregation that night, the anointing of the Lord came upon me. I was holding the book up high as I was proclaiming this word. Suddenly, without any fore-warning, two peals of thunder crashed with great force and a loud noise above the worship center. Because we have a metal roof, we can always tell when it's raining outside during our services. It had not been raining, and the thunder was so loud and dramatic that virtually everyone in the meeting simultaneously stood to their feet, lifted both arms and yelled aloud! I prophesied once more, "Some said it thundered, but it was the voice of God." We all stood there in amazement somewhat dumb-founded. The meeting became much more lively after that, and we had a wonderful night of worship.

Following is the Scripture that the Lord had given me that night to share with the congregation. Here Paul is referring to the evidences of genuineness that accompany true New Testament Christian life and ministry. I am convinced that these characteristics will accompany the kind of Last-Day prophetic ministry within the body of Christ.

> But in all things we commend ourselves as ministers of God: in much patience, in tribulations, in needs, in distresses, in stripes, in imprisonments, in tumults, in labors, in sleeplessness, in fastings; by purity, by knowledge, by longsuffering, by kindness, by the Holy Spirit, by sincere love, by the word of truth, by the power of God, by the armor of righteousness on the right hand and on the left, by honor and dishonor, by evil report and good report; as deceivers, and yet true; as unknown, and yet well known; as dying, and behold we live; as chastened, and yet not killed; as sorrowful, yet always rejoicing; as poor, yet making many rich; as having nothing, and yet possessing all things.
>
> —2 CORINTHIANS 6:4–10

First of all, Paul describes the *negative pressures* that he endured as an anointed apostle of Jesus Christ. Then he refers to the *positive qualities* that were manifested in his character and ministry in the midst of those pressures. Lastly, he rehearses the *paradoxical experiences* that he was called by God to embrace as he walked out his apostolic calling.

Some people actually gravitate to the prophetic ministry because they imagine that if they really learn to hear the Lord's voice with clarity and precision, then they will avoid trials and sufferings. Indeed, we are able to escape unnecessary trials and errors if we live in intimate obedience to the Lord. However, sometimes hearing and obeying the

Lord is the very thing that gets us into trouble in the fallen age. "All who desire to live godly in Christ Jesus will suffer persecution" (2 Tim. 3:12). Paul and Silas were thrown into prison after going to Philippi on the basis of a prophetic vision and performing a miraculous deliverance on a young slave girl. Of course, they also got to experience a supernatural deliverance from that prison by an earthquake sent by God. They then conducted probably the easiest "altar call" in world history for the jailer! We all have a God-ordained "suffering package" that is inescapable as we do the will of God. There are simply things about God's personality that we will not come to know without sufferings and trials.

I once had a spiritual dream of a man walking arrogantly up an aisle of an auditorium. I could read on his sweatshirt a logo that said "No Pain." He turned on his heels, and as he was walking away, I saw God's hand come through the ceiling and slap what appeared to be a bumper sticker on his back. It read, "No Passion." In fact, pain and passion go hand in hand in this life. Pain is very often the crucible in which passion is created in our souls. As challenging as pain can be, it really isn't the great enemy of our souls. We must learn to attain a more redemptive attitude toward legitimate sufferings. This principle and attitude must be vitally embraced by all who would seek to move into the kind of prophetic ministry that is ahead of us. The Lord himself will visit us and form us through these kinds of dealings.

> Come, and let us return to the LORD; for He has torn, but He will heal us; He has stricken, but He will bind us up. After two days He will revive us; on the third day He will raise us up, that we may live in His

sight. Let us know, let us pursue the knowledge of the Lord. His going forth is established as the morning; He will come to us like the rain, like the latter and former rain to the earth.

—HOSEA 6:1–3

I believe that these three categories of experience—pressures (tribulations), virtues and paradoxes—will be the portion of all true apostolic and prophetic ministries—especially as the Last Days come upon the earth. God is already preparing His servants to walk with Him and find Him in these ways.

A SECRET OF PROPHETIC MINISTRY

One night I had dream in which I heard the voice of the Lord. I knew that He was telling me a "secret" about the nature of the prophetic ministry, for which God is jealous. I heard the voice say, "Do you want to know the difference between the religious prophetic and the genuine? Here it is—confidence in God." I understood this to mean that people who desire to move into a higher quality of prophetic ministry must trust the Lord at a very deep level within our souls. The power of the prophetic ministry is not in trying to convince people how profound, relevant or true our words are. It is found in trusting God to give the word, to anoint the word and to establish or fulfill the word. This kind of quality is worth seeking after. I believe that if prophetic ministers will allow the Lord to have His way with us on this level, He will use the power of prophetic ministry to change whole nations as well as to quietly provide a cup of cold water for "little ones" in the name of Jesus Christ.

Father, we place our confidence in You and not in ourselves. Have Your way with us. We are who we are by Your grace. Please release a greater outpouring of the spirit of devotion and a spirit of prophecy upon each person who has opened his or her heart before You to read this book. Grant them the spirit of wisdom and revelation that leads to a deeper experiential intimacy with Jesus Christ. Raise up, for Your honor, thousands of men, women and young people upon whom Your Spirit rests in great measure. Rein in their energies and faculties of spirit, mind and body and reign supreme over them. May they live under the dominion of Your Word and Your Spirit. Send Your holy fire within them, and cause them to burn and shine like human torches— living sacrifices who will display Your excellent glory to all people everywhere. Stir and rouse Yourself like a mighty man, and bare Your arm before the raging nations. Give to the Lamb, through His church's ministry, the reward of His sufferings and the ramifications of His resurrection in this evil age. Let Your kingdom come and Your will be done on earth as it is in heaven. Amen.

Shiloh Ministries

During the time of the judges of Israel, ancient Shiloh was a small town where the tabernacle and the Ark of the Lord were located. It was a place where God's people went to pray and worship before the Lord to seek His face and hear His voice.

In the early 1950s the Lord revealed to Paul Cain His desire to raise up a generation of "nameless and faceless people" who would be a part of a worldwide End-Time revival—ordinary men and women blessed with extraordinary gifts and anointing. In 1997 ninety-four acres in the southern part of Kansas City were purchased to establish a prophetic retreat center that would contribute some way to the fulfillment of this vision of the body of Christ ministering in the fullness of the Holy Spirit and His gifts (Eph. 4:11–13). The ministry of Shiloh, through the grace of God, is committed to the goal of Christians all over the world discerning the prophetic voice of the Lord so as to be thoroughly equipped to strengthen, encourage and comfort others.

For more information on Shiloh Ministries, please visit one of the following Web sites:

Shiloh Ministries: www.shiloh-usa.org
Grace Training Center: www.gtckc.com
Abounding Grace Bookstore: www.abgmcf.com

Or you may contact us at:
SHILOH MINISTRIES
11610 Grandview Road
Kansas City, MO 64137
Fax: (816) 761-0897
E-mail: admin@shiloh-usa.org

As a young pastor not personally inclined toward prophecy, Mike Bickle was taken by surprise by the upsurge of the prophetic gift in his own church. Looking for help and advice, he began a journey away from "prophetic chaos" toward a clearer understanding of God's order. From this experience he wrote *Growing in the Prophetic* with Michael Sullivant to assist in the development of the prophetic ministry in the church today. This book is available from your local Christian bookstore or from Creation House, (800) 599-5750.

You can experience more of God's grace & love!

If you would like free information on how you can know God more deeply and experience His grace, love and power more fully in your life, simply write or e-mail us. We'll be delighted to send you information that will be a blessing to you.

To check out other titles from **Creation House** that will impact your life, be sure to visit your local Christian bookstore, or call this toll-free number:

1-800-599-5750

For free information from Creation House:

CREATION HOUSE
600 Rinehart Rd.
Lake Mary, FL 32746
www.creationhouse.com